A Handbook for

WRITING GRADUATE THESES

by

GOMER POUND

University of Southern Mississippi

KENDALL/HUNT PUBLISHING COMPANY

2460 Kerper Boulevard,
Dubuque, Iowa 52001

Copyright © 1977 by Kendall/Hunt Publishing Company

Library of Congress Catalog Card Number: 77—80739

ISBN 0—8403—1767—0

Printed in the United States of America

401767   01

Preface

Several books have been available to researchers that treat more than adequately scientific method, typology of research, research design, techniques for analyzing data, and formal style of writing. What has not been available is a reference which states succinctly the purposes for each section that might be included in a research report, with criteria given for evaluating the content. To fill this hiatus in literature on research, I prepared for my graduate students what ultimately evolved into this handbook.

My intention was to give these apprentice scholars a convenient guide that could help them write their theses and dissertations by (1) acquainting them section by section with what should be incorporated into their reports, and (2) posing questions about what they wrote of the sort asked by critical readers, typified in their cases by members of graduate examining committees, who should, after all, represent the whole world of scholarship. Frequent cross-referencing between sections of the guide emphasized how tightly knit a thesis can be.

Colleagues and graduate students in other parts of the university soon discovered that the guide helped them in their writing. Its use spread to other campuses. Encouraged by this reception, I wrote the present version, which amplifies the original. By resisting temptations to provide copious examples and illustrations or to digress into matters not concerned directly with writing theses, I preserved my original purpose of providing an easy to consult digest that can be placed beside one's typewriter for quick reference.

The contents are divided into two parts. Part I builds a rationale for research reports. Suggestions for overcoming difficulties usually encountered by beginning writers are incorporated along the way. Chapter 1 sketches the setting for graduate thesis requirements. Chapter 2 points out the importance of a prospectus at the outset of a study and its function as a model for the introductory section in the thesis itself. Chapters 3 through 7 analyze each section of a thesis. Chapter 8 discusses matters that can improve one's informational prose. Chapter 9 explains the abstract, vita, and copyright notice, which often accompany theses.

Part II is the original guide. Its organization parallels that found in

Part I. Purposes are stated for each topic that provide guidance while writing drafts. A student can determine quickly how well these purposes are fulfilled. If more is found than the purposes suggest, the student should look closely for extraneous material. A checklist, which anticipates what critical readers look for, follows each statement of purposes. Once satisfied he has fulfilled the purposes, the writer can use these checklists to evaluate what he has written.

The two parts are complimentary; i.e., they treat the same topics in two different ways for two distinct purposes. Part I is meant to be read before writing begins—preferably, before starting on the study. Part II is designed for quick reference while the thesis is being written.

To emphasize the internal bonds among sections in a research report, the cross-references *q.v.* (which see) and *cf.* (compare) are used liberally. This will, it is hoped, lead users to write tightly integrated theses, despite what at first might seem to be a paradox of self-sufficient sections.

Gomer Pound
University of Southern
Mississippi
February, 1977

Contents

PART I
Rationale for Research Reports

Chapter 1

The Setting for Theses as Requirements for Graduate Degrees

Thesis requirements for graduate degrees are rooted in the origins of the university system itself. Their *raison d'etre* can be understood better when viewed in this perspective.

Students and teachers had become numerous enough by the beginning of the thirteenth century that they organized themselves into guilds. Privileges and charters were sought, both from the Pope and from kings. An association like that of teachers and students was called a *universitas,* a general Roman legal term that was practically equivalent to the modern "corporation." Later the term became restricted to its present meaning.

Universities were primarily places for taking apprenticeship in the Arts. Students could progress from apprentice to journeyman to master. Those who attained the highest rank were certified as proficient to practice the teaching craft. The right to examine and license its own teachers was the most important of a university's privileges.

By the fourteenth century a *baccalaureatus* degree had evolved. Passing a test for this degree compared to advancing from apprentice to journeyman in contemporaneous guilds. Persons holding a baccalaureatus degree might be permitted to assist the master and give some elementary instruction, while at the same time continuing their own studies—a medieval forerunner of a graduate assistantship.

Finally, after hearing a sufficient number of courses, a student could present himself to be examined for the teaching license. His examination took the form of a public trial. The student would select an appropriate subject, contemplate it thoroughly in light of existing scholarship, and arrive at a conclusion about it called his *thesis*. "Thesis" means "a position or proposition that a person (as a candidate for scholastic honors) advances and of-

1

fers to maintain by argument."[1] The student then defended his thesis in scholarly disputation in the presence of the masters and against all comers. If he acquitted himself successfully, he was admitted to the highest rank, and became known as "master," "doctor," or "professor." His oral trial served the same purpose as an examination of representative works submitted by an aspirant to the rank of master in a bootmakers, goldsmiths, or other guild.

The tradition of formulating a thesis to be defended against a company of scholars has carried down to the present. During the intervening time its reason and purpose have become obfuscated for most graduate students. Today, a graduate student is asked to identify a problem within his discipline for investigation. A preliminary gathering of sufficient information related to the problem enables him to formulate a probable solution, called an *hypothesis*. Hypotheses are *tentative* explanations, provisionally accepted to explain certain phenomena. In research studies they serve to bring out and give meaning to the evidence.

A student's problem and his hypothesis, along with supportive and explanatory information, are submitted to a committee of graduate faculty in a proposal to continue the investigation.[2] After receiving approval, the student tests his hypothesis through scholarly research. Any conclusion about his hypothesis derived from this research becomes his *thesis*. Customarily, the student undergoes an oral defense of his thesis before a committee of graduate professors. Other graduate faculty are welcome to attend the defense.

In medieval times a student was not required to write down how he arrived at his thesis. Through the years the practice grew to report the entire scholarly process in writing. "Thesis" gradually came to mean the written report to most students. Taking on this additional meaning pushed the original into the background. *Dissertation,* which has come to mean the written report of a study submitted for a doctoral degree (requiring more depth and quality of scholarship than what is expected at the master's level), is used synonymously with "thesis" in many places. "Dissertation" originally meant simply an extended treatment of a subject, as an essay. *Throughout the remainder of this handbook, "thesis" and "dissertation" will be treated as synonyms.*

Three things become apparent from the foregoing historical sketch. First, research studies are scholarly endeavors which test proposed solutions to problems. Secondly, a thesis requirement is not anachronistic. More than slavish adherence to academic tradition is involved: it demonstrates a stu-

1. *Webster's New Collegiate Dictionary* (Springfield, Massachusetts: G. & C. Merriam, 1976), s.v.
2. Cf. Chapter 2, The Prospectus.

2

dent's independence and worth as a scholar. Finally, "thesis" has a twofold meaning. In terms of a study, it is the conclusion drawn from it—the confirmation or rejection of an hypothesis. In terms of a document, a thesis is a written report—a clear and explicit description of a study, from its inception to its conclusion.

Thesis requirements have taken on a formidable aspect for many novice graduate students due to the nature of the work entailed. The masses of students in the United States are not accustomed to tutorial-type classes, which place them on their mettle as independent scholars. They therefore do not view registering for thesis class as they view registering for other classes. Graduate professors often hear the complaint, "But I don't know how to write a thesis." Aside from a misplaced emphasis on the written report which such protestations demonstrate, their argument is no more tenable than complaints about registering for any other course because one can not at registration time meet course requirements. Should it be known that one already could "write a thesis," he conceivably would not be required to do so.

The manner in which thesis requirements sometimes are handled also contributes to misgivings held by incipient scholars. As with many other classes, one should not enroll for "thesis" unless certain prerequisites have been met in previous courses. Along with an understanding of what research entails (preferably accompanied by practical experience), they include practice in clear, logical thought, practice in writing in scholarly style, and practice in using the style manual adopted by the department. Unfortunately, graduate programs do not always provide these prerequisites. Regardless, a student is cast loose at or near the end of his course work and expected to produce his magnum opus. This handbook has been devised to help overcome part of his perplexity; viz., how to prepare the written report.

Chapter 2

The Prospectus

Writing a prospectus is an important preliminary step for anyone who plans to make a major research study. A prospectus sets forth clearly and succinctly what the investigator proposes to do, and seeks approval for the venture. As a bonus, a prospectus is the prototype of the Introductory Section (q.v.) in the thesis resulting from the study, and is a worthwhile exercise in writing in scholarly style.

Often the importance of a prospectus is not fully understood by inexperienced scholars who, eager to get on with their research, view it as a bothersome, time-consuming chore. On the contrary, writing a prospectus is well worth the effort required when weighed against the frustrations and difficulties that await when a study is not carefully planned before one plunges into data-gathering. Such a sophisticated activity as formal research can not be carried out successfully without a premeditated design.

By the time a prospectus is completed, the researcher will have clarified the exact nature of the problem and how he will set about investigating it. The kinds of data sought and how they will be treated will have been established. Every foreseeable variable, including potential sources of error, will have been anticipated. Graduate students are helped in their planning by advisory committees, whose members apply their corporate knowledge and experience as they examine the prospectus.

An approved prospectus forms a sort of contract between student and faculty. This agreement says, in effect, that the faculty approve the topic and the way in which it will be investigated. Only poor quality research, poor quality reporting, not carrying through as proposed, or someone else completing the same study first, should prevent acceptance of the final report.

Once a prospectus is accepted, approved copies should be filed with each graduate committee member. They can refer to their copies whenever drafts are submitted for review. Minor deviations from the prospectus usually are permitted at the directing professor's discretion. Major changes should be submitted for the entire committee's approval.

A Title (q.v.) and provision for signatures of Approval (q.v.) are the only necessary preliminaries for graduate prospectuses. The format for these two items can differ from that used in the thesis. Each school has its own style regulations.

The body of a prospectus is, in organization and in content, a preliminary version of the Introductory Section that will appear in the thesis, only its tone is adapted to a *proposal* for an undertaking, rather than to a *description* of a *fait accompli*. Since the Introductory Section is discussed in Chapter 4, only those deviations necessitated by the nature of the prospectus will be treated at this point.

"Incidence of the Problem" is a section sometimes placed after Need for the Study (q.v.) in a prospectus to emphasize how prevalent the problem is or to explain how the investigator identified it, although this information can be incorporated neatly into Need for the Study or Background Basic to the Problem (q.v.). "Foreseeable Outcomes," or "Implications of the Study" are captions that can substitute for "Purpose of the Study" (q.v.) when the investigator wants to strengthen his argument for acceptance by emphasizing his proposed study's probable value. "Organization of the Remainder of the Report" (q.v.) ordinarily is omitted; however, the investigator may indicate how he proposes to organize the data-reporting section in the final report, in which case the caption "Proposed Organization of the Report" is appropriate. Although a prospectus is a preliminary version of the first chapter (or chapters) in a thesis, information found during a study will cause revisions and expansions.

Chapter 8, "General Considerations," will help a writer produce a stylistically acceptable document. One remark about tense should be made in view of the tone used in a prospectus. A proposal makes more use of present tense (e.g., "The investigator *proposes to seek* . . .") and future tense (e.g., "Data *will be obtained* . . .") than can be permitted in a thesis. When revised for the final report, tenses are changed to past.[1]

Appendixes (q.v.) that clarify or illustrate the research design might be needed. Models of proposed data-gathering instruments (e.g., questionnaires or tests) or proposed analytical tools can be presented in appendixes.

A prospectus is supported by a Bibliography (q.v.), which can be titled "Supporting Bibliography," "Tentative Bibliography," or given any other caption that indicates its provisional, exploratory nature. Committees do not expect complete bibliographies. They are concerned about

whether enough prior searching has gone into the proposal,

whether the references cited do support the argument for the study, and

whether there will be sufficient material to work with.

1. Cf., Tense, p. 56.

An observation can be made to the beginning researcher about the amount of material represented in both the Bibliography and the Review of Related Literature (q.v.) in a prospectus. If little material has been found, this can support the Need for the Study by pointing out existing gaps in knowledge, *or* it can suggest the problem is not important enough to warrant exhaustive research. On the other hand, a great amount of material can mean the problem has already been thoroughly investigated, *or* it can indicate that further delimitations might be needed.

Some graduate schools require a section on "Personal Qualifications," as a means of assessing the investigator's suitability for carrying the study through successfully. Information about the student's education, including degrees and courses taken, professional experiences, resources available to him, and any other qualifications that fit him for the proposed research are included.[2]

2. Cf., Vita, p. 65.

Chapter 3

Preliminaries

Items included in the preliminary section of a thesis

give the reader a quick overview of the contents,

acknowledge indebtedness for assistance received during the study or while preparing the manuscript, and

provide convenient references to information in the report.[1]

Final drafts of these items, except for the title, are written last. Taking titles, subheadings, and captions directly from the final draft of the body of the thesis assures that they will match exactly.[2] The student may also wish to add expressions of appreciation for assistance in preparing the final copy to his acknowledgments.

Title

A thesis first draws attention through its title. Unlike titles in popular prose, which arouse interest because of what they imply or leave unsaid, a research title arouses interest because its subject is clear. Other scholars might pass over a thesis whose title is not carefully formulated, because they will not see its relevance. Vague or misleading titles can cause other investigators to waste valuable time and money in obtaining reports for study. Good scholars recognize their obligations to other researchers in these matters.

Because they serve a different function, titles for theses often are longer than those given novels or magazine articles. For additional clarification,

1. A practice of permitting dedications to be included in theses has arisen in some schools. Dedications are not required; indeed, they are in questionable taste, because they are personal in nature, not of interest to the reader, and not in keeping with the general character of a research report. If a dedication is included, it appears before the Acknowledgments, and should consist simply of "To" followed by a name.
2. Experienced typists likewise defer preliminaries to last, copying titles, captions, and pagination directly from the finished manuscript.

subtitles sometimes are employed. Subtitles do not always serve their purpose, however, since they frequently are omitted from references and library guides.

While a title can not be sufficiently lengthy to describe adequately a study's problem, data, procedures, and results, it can reflect the study's limits. Features which limit a study in research method or in variables (e.g., population, geography, date) usually should be included. If these features are not significant (e.g., the results can be generalized to other populations, areas, or times), indicating limitations might not be necessary. The following fictitious titles reflect clearly each study's limits.

Lake Washetall, 1974: The Ester Chemical Company's Effect on the Lake Ecosystem

An Historical Analysis of Innovation in American Automobile Manufacture, 1915-1930

A Rhetorical Analysis of John S. Miller's Speeches During His Campaign for Governor of Mississippi, 1970

Important nouns that can serve as key words in subject indexes of journals and library guides form a title's lean core. Other words should be kept to a minimum. Growing utilization of information retrieval systems places additional importance on carefully selected key words under which a title might be indexed. Some models of tightly written titles are:

The Ecology of Ramadoph Pertunae in Wheat

Systems-Oriented Management Practices for Hospitals

James Johnson's Moral Teleology

Key words under which a thesis can be indexed are also important at the time copies are processed into college libraries. When not provided with the information they need, catalogers must read enough of a thesis to decide what subject headings they will use for descriptive cataloging.[3] Many libraries can not afford specialists in all disciplines who can interpret reports correctly, thus creating possibilities that theses might be placed under inappropriate headings and not be found under those an investigator would logically consult. Library of Congress cards ordinarily are not available for these studies.

By all means, broad generalizations and vague or superfluous wording should be stripped from titles. "Some Aspects of . . .," or "Comments

3. An Abstract (q.v.) is helpful for this purpose.

on . . .," are vague generalizations. "A Study of . . .," or "An Investigation of . . .," are superfluous, because they simply state what is expected. When qualified in some manner, "An Historical Study of . . .," "An Experimental Investigation of . . .," they can be acceptable.

Vague: *Four Years as a Change Agent*

Superfluous: *A Study of Characteristics Which Are Associated with . . .*

Better: *Characteristics of . . .*

Superfluous: *A Study to Determine the Suitability of Using Audio Cassette Programs as One Alternate Delivery System for Informing Plant Superintendents of Current Practices and Concepts in Management*

Better: *Informing Plant Superintendents of Current Practices and Concepts in Management Through Audio Cassettes*

The title appears on the title page, along with other items which identify the study: student's name; his institutional connection; place, month, and year of submission; and degree requirement being fulfilled. This compares to a publisher's imprint in a book. The format is set by the style manual or title page sheet adopted by the school.

Approval

Graduate theses are not accepted by graduate schools without signed approvals by authorized persons; viz., major professors, committee members, department chairmen, school deans, or graduate deans. Both place and form for affixing these signatures will be stipulated in the style manual followed by the school.

Acknowledgments

Acknowledgment is appropriate for encouragement, financial aid, permission to use materials, or assistance received from anyone who was helpful during the study or while preparing the manuscript. Only those who render considerable assistance of a nonroutine nature should be mentioned. Acknowledging paid services (e.g., the typist's) is not in order.

Graduate students should recognize contributions, assistance, and support from outside their "immediate academic family." Assistance given by directing professors or graduate committee members is part of their responsibilities, and does not require acknowledgment. Anyone familiar with graduate theses knows that the role played by these people is implicit in the quality of the manuscript.[4]

Long lists of effusive acknowledgments are not in good taste. Brief, simple, and impersonal wording is desirable at all times. Stereotyped references to the patience and forebearing of one's spouse and family, or exaggerated tributes to one's graduate committee are inappropriate.

"Acknowledgments" can substitute for "Preface" (q.v.) when the writer wishes to acknowledge assistance and a Preface is not deemed necessary. If a Preface is used, acknowledgments can be incorporated into it, usually appearing as a closing section.

Preface

Prefaces are used to

describe the particular audience to whom the report is directed,

express the writer's personal interest in the problem,

state the scope, aim, and general character of the study,

identify the limitations of the study, and

explain what the investigator wished to accomplish.

Graduate theses usually do not call for a Preface, because these matters either are treated in the body of the report or are not in keeping with the objectivity that should characterize the research.

Table of Contents

When research reports attain the compass of theses, they require a Table of Contents. A Table is valuable for acquainting readers with the material quickly, and as a convenient reference to information within the paper. By presenting an outline of the text, the Table enables a reader to read faster. In this light, the student must decide how complete an outline he wishes to furnish. The lowest order of headings decided upon to be included must be used consistently; it can not change from chapter to chapter. Because theses ordinarily are not indexed, a Table of Contents assumes more importance as a reference tool.

---

4. That is why graduate faculty are particular about the quality of work that bears their signatures.

In addition to functioning as an outline for his readers, the Table of Contents is useful to the writer as a synopsis of the report's design and structural pattern. Examining the Table can reveal whether logical organization has been followed. One can see where he has placed (or misplaced) emphasis. In actual practice, most writers produce better reports by making an outline *before* starting to write. The Table of Contents then evolves as a refined version of the working outline.[5]

Titles and headings should be brief, but self-explanatory in terms of the report. They are most effective if built around important nouns, with other words kept to a minimum. When captions of the same level of importance begin with the same grammatical construction the reader can follow the outline of thought more easily.

Giving the typist the Table of Contents without page numbers requires her to take pagination directly from the final copy. All titles and headings should also be copied from the finished typescript, with typists instructed in the lowest order of headings to be included. By following through the paper page by page, a typist can assure that the Table of Contents is accurate. The number of times discrepancies and inaccuracies are found in finished manuscripts suggests that this advice can not be taken lightly. It is surprisingly easy to rewrite, add, or delete captions, perhaps several times, without these changes finding their way back to the preliminaries.

Lists of Tables, Figures, and Illustrations

Data presented in tables, figures, graphs, charts, maps, or photographs should be referenced by page numbers in lists following the Table of Contents (q.v.). Each type of display is placed in a separate list under an appropriate caption, if enough are included in the thesis (ten is a good rule-of-thumb); however, a table may not be listed as an illustration or an illustration be listed as a table. Charts, maps, graphs, sketches, drawings, and diagrams may be labeled as *figures*. Any illustrative materials consisting of a full page or more of paper different from the rest of the thesis, including photographs, whether mounted or full-page size, are designated as *plates*.

Captions are built around important nouns, with other words kept to a minimum. Each should be self-explanatory in its meaning within the context of the thesis.

This: Totals and Percentages of Copper Ions in Sample A

Not this: Totals and Percentages

5. Cf., "Organization of the Thesis," p. 46ff.

Parallel construction, which facilitates following a line of thought, is particularly important for captions in these lists, which sometimes contain long series of related items. It is easier to adjust for parallelism here during final drafts, then make revisions in the body of the thesis, than to try to retain parallelism when constructing tables and illustrations while writing the report. Captions of the same order which are related by a common idea are placed into parallel construction by virtue of that idea, whether they appear consecutively or not: "Percentages of . . .," "Amino Acids Found in . . .," "t-Ratios of . . ."

Remarks about copying pagination and captions directly from the finished copy given earlier apply equally to these lists.

Chapter 4

Introductory Section

Information presented in the Introductory Section is arranged into three groupings. First, the problem and its background are described. Next, the reader is apprised of the procedures followed in studying the problem. Finally, indication is given of what will be found in the remainder of the report.

Sections which describe the problem include: Background Basic to the Problem, Statement of the Problem, Need for the Study, Purpose of the Study, Scope and Delimitations, Basic Assumptions, Statement of the Hypothesis, and Review of Related Literature. Those concerned with procedures are: Nature and Sources of Data, Method of Research, Research Techniques, and Procedures. Definition of Terms, List of Abbreviations and Organization of the Remainder of the Report advise what follows.

Nothing is sacrosanct about either the sequence or the captions for subsections prescribed here. Variations may be made within the three main parts of the Introductory Section according to the nature of the individual study. Some subsections may be omitted if not deemed appropriate. Other headings can be substituted. Alternatives are suggested in the guide which forms Part II of this handbook. The sequence followed here, and the captions suggested, have been chosen as being generally most appropriate. Logical organization and explicit expression provide justification for variations.

Drawing up the final draft of the Introductory Section is left until the rest of the report has been finished.[1] Minor revisions often are necessitated by information in the body of the text.

Background Basic to the Problem

A mistake commonly made by researchers is to assume that their readers know more about the subject than they actually do. Because a reader's interest in the study is aroused by his general understanding of the problem area, does not mean he is as well-informed in the basic setting as the

1. The Prospectus (q.v.), it will be recalled, formed the first draft.

reporter. Not only has the investigator been preoccupied with the specific problem, but his report is written *after* he becomes an authority on the subject. One can easily forget that others are not well-acquainted with the topic after being engrossed for some time with all aspects of the data. Research writers are frequently admonished, "Never overestimate your reader's knowledge; never underestimate his intelligence." A Background Basic to the Problem begins counteracting immediately any tendency toward losing sight of the reader's orientation.

The Background Basic to the Problem can vary in length according to the nature of the problem area, but is kept brief. Good scholars quickly acquaint the reader with the setting, then proceed to the Statement of the Problem (q.v.) as directly as possible.

Confusing Background Basic to the Problem with Need for the Study (q.v.), Purpose of the Study (q.v.), or Review of Related Literature (q.v.) is common among inexperienced researchers. Such confusion can be avoided by breaking the problem statement into its component parts, then commenting briefly on each in the Background. For illustration, possible questions whose answers might orient the reader quickly are suggested for these hypothetical problems.

> *Problem:* To determine why patients admitted to the Honeywood Narcotics Treatment Program leave before completing their treatment plan.
>
> *Questions:* What are the dimensions of the narcotics problem (particularly of drugs treated at Honeywood)?
> Is early departure common to all narcotics treatment programs?
> What and where is Honeywood? How long has its program been in operation?
> What, briefly, is the program (particularly, what are its unique features)?
> How are patients referred (courts, voluntary)?
> How many patients have been admitted? How many have not completed the program?
>
> *Problem:* To determine how John Springer handled didatic messages in his novels so that readers can absorb them without sensing they are reading a philosophical treatise.
>
> *Questions:* Who is (was) John Springer?
> What has he written?
> Which of his writings are generally acknowledged to have philosophical overtones?

The Background Basic to the Problem can appear as the opening statement in the first chapter without a caption. Many will prefer this format, because formal style generally does not permit a caption to follow a title without an intervening text. Some reporters prefer to omit this section and state the problem immediately. The author favors the brief orientation provided by the Background. It also makes a nice transition from the Title (q.v.) to the Statement of the Problem.

Statement of the Problem

The Statement of the Problem is a precise statement of *what* was studied—a more specific rewording of the Title (q.v.). It raises the basic research question, which ultimately is answered by the Conclusions (q.v.).

Formulating a trenchant problem statement is the initial step in any research study; yet, lack of an incisive statement, or confusion of Statement of the Problem with Purpose of the Study (q.v.) or Method of Research (q.v.) constitute common weaknesses in theses. Research literature abounds with problem statements that begin, "The purpose of this study was. . . ." With few exceptions, problem and purpose are separate aspects of a study. The purpose is what was hoped to be achieved by resolving the problem.

Problem statements beginning, "This study compared . . .," suggest a confusion of the problem with the method of solving it. "The problem was to analyze . . ." illustrates another example of confusing research method with the problem, unless the problem itself was to find a technique for analysis. To simply compare, or examine, or analyze suggests the researcher has engaged in fact-finding without interpreting his findings to arrive at conclusions. Mere data-treatment is not enough for studies suitable for theses. To quote Hillway, "Not the facts alone, but the conclusions that we can draw from them, must be regarded as the chief objective of research."[2]

A good test for a problem statement is to see if it can be recast as a research question. This should cause it to revert to the basic question underlying the research. As a further test, the student can ask himself, "What will the answer to this research question reveal?" The answer should duplicate his original problem statement. If not, the answer is itself recast into a research question, and the procedure is continued until two consecutive answers are the same. Two examples will illustrate the test. In the first, an investigator set out to find what effects one substance might have on certain properties of another.

1. *Original problem statement:* The problem of this study was to

2. Tyrus Hillway, *Introduction to Research* (Boston: Houghton Mifflin Co., 1956), p. 119.

17

determine the effects of subsifridines on the electronic distribution of pyroxenide molecules.

2. *Original problem statement recast as a research question:* What are the effects of subsifridines on the electronic distribution of pyroxenide molecules?

3. *Test question:* What will the answer to this research question reveal? *Answer:* It will reveal the effects of subsifridines on the electronic distribution of pyroxenide molecules.

The answer to the test question matches the problem statement; therefore, the original problem statement is valid.

The second example illustrates how a true problem statement sometimes must be uncovered. One kind of study, popular in the field of Education, pits a method of teaching which incorporates experimental variables against a "conventional" method. What follows is a typical application of the test procedure.

1. *Original problem statement:* The purpose [sic] of this study was to compare two methods of teaching English to disadvantaged third-grade students.

2. *Original problem statement recast as a research question:* Although this statement does not lend itself readily to being recast as a question—a good indication it is not a true problem statement—a fair transformation would be, "How do these two methods compare?"

3. *Test question:* What will the answer to this research question reveal? *Answer:* It will reveal whether one method is more effective than the other (unless mere fact-finding is intended). This is obviously not the basic issue, nor does it duplicate the problem statement.

4. *Test answer recast as a research question:* Is one method more effective than the other?

5 *Test question:* What will the answer to this research question reveal? *Answer:* It will reveal whether the experimental variables are more effective for teaching English to disadvantaged third graders than conventional methods. This statement does not duplicate the previous test answer.

6. *Test answer recast as a research question:* Are the experimental

variables more effective for teaching English to disadvantaged third graders than conventional methods?

7. *Test question:* What will the answer to this research question reveal? *Answer:* It will reveal whether the experimental variables are more effective for teaching English to disadvantaged third graders than conventional methods. This statement does match the previous test answer.

8. *True problem statement:* The problem of this study was to determine whether the experimental variables [they should be identified specifically] are more effective for teaching English to disadvantaged students than conventional methods. (It will probably have been discovered by this point that "third-grade students" was only a *delimitation* of a larger problem that permitted the phenomenon to be studied more precisely.)

Problems deal with one essential goal; nevertheless, some can be divided into subproblems, which lead ultimately to subconclusions. When this is the case, a list of subproblem statements, or a list of subquestions to be answered, is presented to the reader. The test applied to the problem statement can be used for statements of subproblems.

Need for the Study

This section enhances the Statement of the Problem (q.v.) by pointing out *why* existing knowledge should be refined, revised, or extended by studying the problem. Needs can range from satisfying the investigator's own curiosity to finding answers to immediate and crucial social or scientific problems. They may or may not be justified in pragmatic terms like comfort and well-being, health, or profit: truth is worth discovering for its own sake. The reader will be in a better position to understand the study and its relationship to the world at large by learning the value of finding answers to the problem.

Purpose of the Study

The Purpose of the Study states the use to which a satisfactory resolution of the problem might be put. Often it will be necessary to combine the study with others to achieve a larger purpose, but the study constitutes a step in that direction. A cogently stated Need for the Study (q.v.) helps the reader perceive the purpose clearly. Logically, the purpose is to satisfy the need, at least in part.

19

More often than not, Purpose of the Study is confused with Statement of the Problem (q.v.). This is understandable; plainly, one makes the study to solve the problem. The Purpose of the Study, however, should answer for the reader, "What, specifically, does the investigator hope might be accomplished by answering the basic research question?" Perhaps there are studies whose purpose and problem are one. When this appears to be the case, a more penetrative analysis usually reveals they are not. This example illustrates how need, purpose, and problem are closely related, yet distinctive, aspects of a study.

Need: To smooth out the seasonal pattern of turkey production. (This relates the turkey industry to the world of economics, marketing, labor.)

Purpose: To investigate the impact that changes in processing and storing can have on turkey production. (This hopes to contribute in one way to smoothing out the seasonal pattern.)

Problem: To determine the minimum-cost schedule for processing and storing turkeys. (This purports to study thoroughly a specific aspect of processing and storing, which in turn might have a bearing on changes that can help smooth out the seasonal pattern.)

Purpose can also become confused with problem when an end product is already in view. For example, a student might have in mind a book that he wishes to write. His research *problem* is not to write the book; rather, it is to identify those elements that should be incorporated into it. The *need* for his study is the reason for producing a book. His *purpose* is to produce a book because of the perceived need. Any book which he should write would be an outgrowth of the study.

Scope and Delimitations

A problem is given sharper definition by establishing the study's limits. Carefully stating what will be *included* and what will be *excluded* helps the reader focus precisely on the matter at hand. The Scope and Delimitations also provides a safeguard against generalizing the Conclusions (q.v.) to larger populations than are warranted by the data, or making premature Recommendations (q.v.).

Critical readers who might wonder about matters or data that are related to the problem but were not intended to be included in the study, are advised in this section what the investigation's exact boundaries were. Thus, the Scope and Delimitations quite specifically extends the admonition against promising more than the investigation attempted to fulfill first encountered in the discussion of the Title (q.v.). Potentially embarassing questions that might weaken an oral defense of a thesis—which typifies passing inspection before the whole world of critical judgment—are parried by citing the study's specific limits. An investigator can not reasonably be held responsible for answering questions that do not fall within the study's purview, although he may offer an informed *opinion*, which is quite another matter.[3]

To set up the Scope and Delimitations while writing his Prospectus (q.v.), an investigator must attempt to foresee every aspect of the proposed venture that will prevent whatever conclusions might evolve from being generalized beyond the parameters under which his study will be made. This calls for him to specify exactly

the portion to be studied of the total data available,

the variables to be isolated for study, and

the relationships to be studied among the variables to be isolated.

Then the question must be asked, "Is there any possibility that the evidence might differ if these data were to be obtained

from a different period in *time* (or over a shorter or longer duration),

from a different *location,*

from a different *population,* or

from a different *environment* (including both physical and social conditions)?"

All variables that might be affected should data be obtained under different conditions must be described as they will be constituted in the study. Experiments carried out in the physical sciences might require few or no delimitations, whereas studies in the social sciences ordinarily have many variables that could be affected by circumstances of time, location, population, or environment.

Once the investigation is underway, minor adjustments often become necessary. These will be incorporated into the Scope and Delimitations that appears in the thesis. All delimitations should be settled upon as early as possible.

3. In this connection, the reporter should confine himself strictly to his data, and refrain assiduously from making statements that can not be supported by the information at hand. Extrapolations and inferences must be clearly labeled, should any reason be found for including them. Cf., p. 46.

Basic Assumptions

Assumptions are precepts that are accepted as operational for purposes of the research. Those that underlie the data's

nature (e.g., "This sample is typical of the total population."),

analysis (e.g., "This tool will, in fact, measure what it purports to measure when applied to these data."), or

interpretation (e.g., "This criterion is valid when applied to these findings.")

must be delineated. If a reader will not accept the assumptions basic to the research, there is no reason for him to continue, because they influence the entire endeavor. In particular, identification of assumptions provides a basis for formulating a Statement of the Hypothesis (q.v.), and for interpreting information resulting from the study. Later, assumptions will give meaning and value to the Conclusions (q.v.), and lend credence to the Recommendations (q.v.).

Some assumptions are facts or principles that are generally accepted by informed people. A statement that water will run downhill, e.g., hardly needs substantiating evidence. Others may be founded upon previous research. An assumption based upon certain previous research might be accepted by some scholars, but not by others. In that event, the investigator should state clearly which position he adopts. Still other assumptions are made, indeed must be made, because with the resources of information, time, and research techniques at his disposal, the investigator could not proceed otherwise. An assumption that people who respond to a questionnaire will answer honestly is an example.

Any research assumption should be tenable, in keeping with existing knowledge, and preferably supported by other research. Although a researcher is not expected to prove his basic assumptions, he is responsible for an acceptable rationale for them.

Statement of the Hypothesis

At this point in his report the investigator posits an answer to the Statement of the Problem (q.v.) in the form of an hypothesis. Chapter 1 brought out that an hypothesis is an *hypo*thesis; i.e., a *tentative* explanation placed under known facts or observable phenomena to explain them.[4] Once tested (the reason for the research), the hypothesis is either confirmed or rejected,

4. Cf., p. 2.

usually in terms qualified by the Scope and Delimitations (q.v.) or by the adequacy of the data. To the extent it is proven tenable, the hypothesis becomes a thesis.

As proposed solutions, hypotheses can not be wildly speculative, based upon fanciful wishes, or show unfounded bias. They are predicated from known facts and Basic Assumptions (q.v.).[5] Considerable thought and study about the problem area are requisites for arriving at an hypothesis.

Well-formulated and well-stated hypotheses are as simple, clear, and concise as it is possible to refine them. Teamed with a tightly drawn Scope and Delimitations, the hypothesis becomes a directional beam for the study. No other force is as strong in unifying a report. All evidence is adduced for the purpose of supporting or refuting the argument advanced by the hypothesis: digressions to peripheral or irrelevant matters become obvious.

In the discussion of Statement of the Problem, it was noted that a problem might be broken into subproblems.[6] This can be true with hypotheses as well. The major hypothesis is proposed as the answer to the major problem. Corollary hypotheses are suggested as answers to subproblems.

Hypotheses are not found in all theses, although when not stated forthrightly they usually are implied in problem statements, purposes, or objectives. If fact-finding is the sole purpose, an hypothesis might not be required, but major studies should involve interpretation of the facts to answer research questions.

Review of Related Literature

An investigator is expected to have searched out all literature related to his problem. In this section he presents precis of pertinent literature he has examined. A Review of Related Literature can illuminate every aspect of a problem by

erecting an historical framework for it;

describing its present status;

showing that existing evidence does not solve the problem adequately;

presenting specific ideas and opinions of others (including diverse and contrary views);

supporting the purpose of the study;

proposing useful theoretical constructs for the research; and,

5. Cf., Background Basic to the Problem, p. 15, and Review of Related Literature, p. infra.
6. Cf., p. 19.

adverting comparative references that assist in analyzing the data and interpreting the results.

Clearly, this review is as important to the reader in understanding the thesis
as it was to the researcher during the study. More than an historical
background for the problem is provided. A perceptive review becomes a po-
tent unifying element through its interrelationships with other sections.

Critical readers view thoroughness of search and adequacy of presentation as indicative of the merit of the entire study. A scholar should take
pains that his review demonstrates a comprehensive grasp of the problem
and an awareness of recent developments. Except in unusual circumstances,
only research studies are reviewed. Scholarly investigations are quests for
truth; therefore, based upon fact.

Papers of thesis proportion frequently have separate chapters devoted to
the Review of Related Literature, due to the number of closely related
studies. Separate chapters are placed immediately after the rest of the introductory material.

When several precis are presented, they should be grouped by similarity
of content, or by type of contribution each makes to the study. Briefly sum-
marizing each group, pointing out its significance, will make the review
more effective.

Nature and Sources of Data

Consistent with the Introductory Section's function as preparation for
what follows, it is good practice to describe in a general way the nature of
the data treated and the sources from which they were drawn. Appropos of
their nature, a brief description of the kinds treated and the forms in which
they were found will suffice. In regard to sources, the reader should be told
where, when, and from whom data were obtained, with clear differentiation
made among those drawn from primary, secondary, or tertiary sources.
Detailed descriptions will be found when data are presented later in the
report. Only previews are needed at this point.

Method of Research

Most research studies fall into basic types; e.g., historical, descriptive,
analytical, experimental, or philosophical. Each type suggests differences in
purposes, kinds of data sought, and treatments to which data are subjected.
Those acquainted with the typology of research can follow better the
Presentation, Analysis, and Interpretation of Data (q.v.) when informed *a
priori* of the research method employed. Codifying research into categorical
types has resulted in generally accepted criteria for sound methodology in

each; thus, the reader is given another tool for evaluating the intrinsic merit of the study before being confronted with the bulk of data.

Research Techniques

Each type of research utilizes techniques that are best suited to it. A statement about the research techniques employed during the study should follow identification of the kind of research undertaken to solve the problem. Often this statement is included in the Method of Research (q.v.).

Procedures

Having established the kind of research undertaken and the techniques employed, the investigator then summarizes the procedures that were followed. A more detailed account is found in the Presentation, Analysis, and Interpretation of Data (q.v.), but the reader should be given a preview of the steps taken during the study. This discussion, along with Research Techniques (q.v.), can be incorporated into one section with the Method of Research (q.v.).

Definition of Terms

Explicit statement, an overriding desideratum in reporting research, is difficult to achieve, because words have connotative as well as denotative meanings, are often used loosely in other forms of communication, or even within a discipline, and frequently have more than one accepted definition. To limit possibilities of misinterpretation or misunderstanding, key words that are

subject to more than one interpretation,

open to the application of connotative, rather than denotative, meanings,

unusual in any way,

technical, or

coined by the researcher

should be defined precisely as the reporter intends to use them before their appearance in the Presentation, Analysis, and Interpretation of Data (q.v.). Once defined, terms should be used only in their established meanings throughout the remainder of the thesis.

One should be prepared to cite authority for definitions others might disagree with. Obscure, unusual, or rare meanings should be avoided. Terms coined by the researcher should be logically contrived, with eyery effort made to eschew cumbersome, awkward, or superfluous wording.

List of Abbreviations

Scholarly writing, emphasizing clear expression, exact meanings, and formal style, does not lend itself to abbreviations, employing them only when terms or references are used frequently or when they are found commonly in other writing styles.[7] Even then, one should be prudent in their selection. Spelling out terms can not be incorrect.

Abbreviations arrange themselves into three general categories:

those that are understood by a wide readership, such as those used in measurement (qt., Dec., mm), formal writing (e.g., i.e., viz.), or titles (Mr., Dr.);

those that are recognized within academic disciplines (ANOVA, HAM, CAI);

those that are originated by the investigator for the purposes of his report.

Most abbreviations that fall within the first category are spelled out (the style manual adopted by the school will give instructions); those in the second and third categories require explanation.

All abbreviations must be orthodox and employed in consistent form. Those devised by the investigator should be logically derived from the terms they represent and readily understood by a reader who has not seen them before.

Abbreviations are used for convenience and simplicity. Whenever number, similarities, or complexities of abbreviations impair clear communication in any way, the list should be revised.

No abbreviation that requires explanation in the List of Abbreviations should be found prior to this section. Once decided upon, an abbreviation should substitute for the term it represents from this point onward, with complete spelling reintroduced only as might be required to conform with formal style, as, e.g., with the initial word in a sentence, or in quoted material.

7. In footnotes, bibliographies, and tables, abbreviations are not only permissable, but are preferred.

Organization of the Remainder of the Report

Many researchers advocate giving a synopsis of what will be encountered in the ensuing sections of their theses at the end of the introductory chapter (a practice recommended by the author). Brief statements about the contents of each subsequent chapter suffice. The intent is not to anticipate actual data, but to sensitize the reader to the way in which material he will be reading is organized. Coupled with the outline already provided by the Table of Contents (q.v.), a preview is given that assists the reader in following the discourse.

Chapter 5

Presentation, Analysis, and Interpretation of Data

This section is the heart of a thesis. Here readers discover how facts were coalesced into evidence that was brought to bear on the problem. Because the evidence must be developed in whatever order is best suited to the data, this section, unlike the other main divisions, does not follow a prescribed arrangement of subsections.

Presentation and Analysis of Data

The researcher should describe exactly

what data were collected, where and how they were located, and how and in what form they were obtained;

what steps were taken to validate all data, and what safeguards were made against possible errors in collecting and organizing the evidence;

what analytical treatments were given the data (with reasons for choosing the particular treatments made clear);

what equipment or apparatus was used in the study.

One question will reveal whether a thesis is sufficiently explicit about the data and adequately descriptive of their treatment; viz., **Could another investigator replicate the study with the information given and understand clearly why each step was taken?** Any "blank spots" revealed by this question must be filled with more detail.

All relevant data used to test the hypothesis are recounted in these chapters. No alternative explanations, no adverse evidence can be glossed over or excluded. Any gaps in the evidence or sources of possible error should be pointed out. A case must be developed that demonstrates that the evidence actually does substantiate the Conclusions (q.v.).

Recognizing during his study the difficulties inherent in remaining objective about one's own research, the investigator must have attempted resolutely to refute his own suppositions. If he has done so, he is in a better position to anticipate what information is needed to answer questions his readers might raise.

Quotations

Direct quotation is justifiable whenever it is important to preserve exact wording or characteristic language, but should be used sparingly. Long or frequent quotations interrupt thought flow and raise questions about whether the writer has absorbed the ideas represented well enough to incorporate them into his own thinking. Quotations can be reduced in length and in number by

paraphrasing the essential ideas:

selecting excerpts judiciously from the entire quotation, with ellipses indicating omissions, or with the excerpts run into a paraphrase of the remainder of the text;

presenting the gist of what was said, with the reader referred to the complete text in an Appendix (q.v.).

All three treatments require appropriate documentation. Style manuals give intructions for the mechanical treatment of quoted material.

Tabulation and Display of Data

Tables and similar nonparagraph displays of data can make otherwise hopelessly complicated presentations intelligible. Three conventions should be followed unvaryingly when they are used. First, each display is introduced in the text and clearly identified by title and number. Next, the display is placed as close as physically possible to its first mention (style manuals give instructions on this). Lastly, the writer comments on the data's significance.

The first two steps present little difficulty, aside from mechanical problems associated with placing the display into the final copy. The third step—*commenting* about the data—gives inexperienced writers trouble. Most often, they simply repeat bits of information from the display. There is no justification for giving sophisticated readers specific data in a display, then repeating it for them in the text. This borders on insulting their intelligence. One or the other statement is sufficient, and the display should have been chosen because it presents data more effectively.

Appropriate comments come more easily once the writer realizes that each display only *presents* data; whoever examines the display must *interpret* the information. Viewed in this light, one type of comment can be seen as generalizations distilled from the data that the writer wants to be certain the reader notes, because they are particularly important to the discussion. Other comments can relate specific information or ideas represented in the display to information or ideas found elsewhere in the thesis, pointing out the significance these relationships have for the problem. Through reading these comments, the reader can grasp the main ideas without studying the display. The information is there if he wishes to confirm or challenge any interpretations the researcher has drawn.

Illustrations

Illustrative materials—charts, graphs, diagrams, photographs—do not display data, they *facilitate understanding* data. Formerly these materials were viewed as *supplementing* the text, and were used sparingly. The present view is that such material can *supplant* text. A researcher need not be hesitant about using illustrations to make his discussion more comprehensible, although when used only to stimulate interest they still have no place in scholarly papers. The three steps followed in treating displays are followed with illustration.

Interpretation of Data

Unfortunately, many research tyros think their task is complete once they have analyzed their data. This is not enough. Such a misconception can lead to meaningless analysis, or overanalysis. Worse yet, it can result in "conclusions" that are not conclusions at all, but mere iterations of the findings.[1]

Meanings must be extracted from these findings that enable the investigator to answer questions raised by the hypothesis. Explanations must be given for all facts that emerge from the analysis. Relationships must be pointed out among these facts. Implications of this new information when juxtaposed with facts already abstracted from other studies in the Review of Related Literature (q.v.) need exploration.

An objective search for logical meanings in the facts surfacing from the analysis leads to interpretations of the findings that are called to the reader's attention. Insightful interpretations become original thought, the essential product of research.

Organization of the Data

Two basic principles are used to organize the development of the evidence. Combining the two forms a third, and perhaps more effective, ap-

1. Cf., p. 35.

31

proach. The first principle is to organize according to *chronology*. The second is to organize according to *topic*.

Because a thesis is a report of a study, a diary of the actual events in their order of occurrence makes a logical organization. This suggestion is given advisedly. More often than researchers like to admit, events do not occur during an investigation in their most fortuitous sequence. Unforeseen problems, unexpected delays, unanticipated events have a way of upsetting the most carefully planned research designs. As a consequence, following a chronology can actually mean placing the description into a logical succession, accompanied by any explanations as to why the real sequence occurred, or how any chronological abberations might have affected the findings.

The topical approach enables one to present complex ideas in a way that the data itself usually dictates as most logical. Building from the particular to the general, e.g., is an effective arrangement—usually more appropriate for research studies than moving from the general to the particular. Each point can be discussed in turn, with appropriate data adduced. The points themselves can be arranged in the best order of logic and importance. Step by step, minor points can lead to major, answers to subhypotheses lead to answers to the main hypothesis. An effective psychology for the complicated ideas found in research reports is to present the whole idea, develop it in its details, then synthesize these details into the whole once again. Cause-to-effect is another arrangement that works well with information from experiments, or from studies in the social sciences.

As a generalization, the chronological approach might be best suited for describing the data-gathering and arrangement processes, the topical approach for analyzing and interpreting the data. The two can be interchanged throughout the main body of the thesis.

Interpretations of the findings can occur concomitantly with the analyzation. This is the practice most widely followed. An alternative is to present and analyze all data, then follow with interpretations.

Organization of the evidence into chapters and sections will be dictated by

the amount of information,

the relative importance of the information, and,

the plan adopted for presenting the information.

Additional advice on organization is found in Chapter 8.[2]

2. Cf., pp. 46ff.

Chapter 6

Concluding Section

Many read the concluding sections of theses first. Usually they are interested in the Conclusions. They might even use the conclusions without reading or fully comprehending the data, accepting the research on faith that it was done responsibly. The Summary provides them with a brief description of the entire study. Recommendations gives suggestions for action. Limitations of the Study cautions against ill-advised interpretations or applications of the results. If, after examining the concluding section, the reader wishes to read more, he can turn to other sections.

Items in the concluding section are usually incorporated into one chapter. *No new data are admissable in the concluding section.*

The end of the Summary (the first item) concludes the account of the investigation. It also ends the portion of the thesis in which the investigator must exhibit detached objectivity and treat data factually. This in no way implies that he can suddenly show bias or state opinions, or is no longer required to base statements on fact. Nonetheless, once an investigator begins to draw conclusions from his findings, he becomes subjective to the degree that his own interpretations are imposed. Two people can look at the same facts and draw different conclusions.

Recommendations likewise exhibits subjective elements, because it is one person's ideas for courses of action. Limitations of the Study, which directs attention to actual occurrences, is less subjective.

Summary

The Summary is a synopsis of the preceding chapters. Analysis of previous text is permissable only insofar as it points up agreements, differences, or interrelationships. Writing final summaries is made easier when each preceding chapter, exclusive of the first, has been summarized.[1] A summary of the introductory material and precis of chapter summaries are synthesized into this higher order summary. If chapter summaries have not been used, the final summary consists of a brief account of the important

1. Cf., p. 48.

ideas in each chapter. A well-constructed Table of Contents (q.v.) furnishes a ready-made outline. Conversely, writing the Summary gives the student an opportunity for an internal check on his Table of Contents.

A mistake found frequently in summaries is that they simply recall data, rather than summarize. Although lengths vary with the content of individual theses, once a summary extends beyond two typewritten pages the student should suspect he has lapsed into repetition of data. Another criticism is that all too often summaries introduce new material. The caution against including anything not previously stated merits reemphasis.[2]

The Summary can be tested by asking a colleague who is not familiar with the project to read it, then tell what he thinks was the problem studied, how it was studied, and what results were obtained (he should not see the thesis title). This test reveals quickly how well the investigator can state succinctly what his study was about.

Conclusions

Conclusions are the climaxes of theses. Readers discover to what extent questions posed by the Statement of the Hypothesis (q.v.) have been answered, or, to be more precise, to what extent the hypothesis is sustained—it is not unusual for hypotheses to be accepted with qualifications. Ideally, the weight of evidence and logic of reasoning will have lead inexorably to indisputable confirmation of the hypothesis, but it is not always possible to construct such overwhelming proof. Data can be incomplete or inconclusive, or explain only part of the problem. Conclusions will fall somewhere along a continuum extending from complete rejection to complete acceptance.[3]

Drawing more conclusions than the data can support is a common error. Research tyros sometimes seem to struggle to milk every possible conclusion they can from their data, usually at the expense of drawing ambiguous or erroneous ones. Perhaps they feel, mistakenly, that a surfeit of conclusions will testify that they were meticulous in their work, or they may simply exhibit a natural inclination to derive maximum return from exhaustive efforts. Whatever the reason, an inflated list of conclusions demonstrates they do not understand the teleological influence of hypotheses that should pervade the entire investigation. Responses to hypotheses are all that is expected. The main conclusion is the response to the main hypothesis. Subhypotheses are spoken to with subconclusions. Occasionally there will

2. Cf., p. 33.

3. Finding that their hypotheses can not be accepted upsets most students. They must recognize that proving something does *not* solve the problem represents a contribution to knowledge, if this has not been demonstrated before.

be instances in which serendipitous findings lead to conclusions not sought by the hypothesis. These are admissable, of course.

Another fault frequently encountered in this section is that what purportedly are conclusions actually summarize or repeat data. "Conclusions" like this can be found throughout the literature: "The scores made by the control group and the experimental group were very similar." Aside from the weakness that "very similar" does not tell much of anything, the statement merely recalls a finding derived from analyzing the data. This finding needs to be interpreted in a way that will lead to a conclusion about what it means in terms of an answer to the problem.

Conclusions must not be generalized beyond what the data can support. It is advisable to reconsult the Scope and Delimitations (q.v.) as a check against this error. All too often studies done with limited populations report conclusions in ways that lead people to think they are universally true. Only additional research can substantiate such assertions. Conclusions can not be based on assumptions or implications derived from the data, either. Although these constraints might seem to diminish the importance of what they can conclude, beginning researchers should remember that they have in all probability attempted to thoroughly study only a small bit of what is yet to be known. If they do this well, they can be pleased with their efforts.

A study can be valid in every way, yet two readers can draw divergent conclusions because they interpret the data differently. For this reason, the student should reread his Basic Assumptions (q.v.) to see if they were stated adequately in respect to any influence they might exert on interpretations given the findings. For example, an investigator who measures the intonational (pitch) characteristics of clarinets and finds that most tones have a tendency to be sharp to the widely accepted pitch standard of A440 cycles per second might conclude that manufacturers build these musical instruments too sharp. Another observer might justifiably conclude that clarinets are not built too sharp, but are designed to be tuned higher than A440 cycles per second. It depends upon one's position (basic assumption) on the matter of A440 cycles per second, which, it can be remarked, is a moot issue among practicing musicians.

Recommendations

In this section the investigator can suggest possible actions to be taken as a result of his findings. Whether hypotheses are proven to be valid or invalid, possible courses to be pursued might be indicated. The first chapter includes a Need for the Study (q.v.), which precedes a Purpose of the Study (q.v.). Recommendations can relate directly to fulfilling the purpose for which the study was undertaken, which in turn will help overcome the need to be satisfied.

Recommendations for new or further research are frequently generated during the course of an investigation. Such recommendations can be particularly valuable to other scholars who are seeking ideas for research topics. New research might be pursued along lines of inquiry opened by the study or which occured to the investigator, but which fell outside the Scope and Delimitations (q.v.). Unforeseen questions or problems that did fall within the circumscriptions of the study, but which had to be left unresolved, also prompt suggestions for further research. These data gaps no doubt weakened the study and probably caused qualifications in the acceptance of the hypothesis; consequently, their resolution is important to the problem area.

As with Conclusions (q.v.), caution must be exercised that recommendations are based upon findings, not upon opinion. Care must be taken that they are not stated in terms that make them sound like conclusions. Recommendations should not be generalized beyond the scope of the study. They also should not be made without duly considering their possible consequences, or taking into account their practicality or feasibility. If no recommendations are warranted, none should be given.

Limitations of the Study

This section calls attention to conditions or events that prevented the study from being as perfect as could be wished. Uncontrollable circumstances should be explained, and their possible implications pointed out. Methods or data which proved of relatively little value should be noted. Reading this section will help other researchers avoid the same pitfalls. The Limitations of the Study can be written as if advising a colleague who is about to start on a similar study how he can profit from the investigator's experience.

Pointing out a study's limitations also helps others interpret the thesis properly. The investigator is obligated to mention contradictions, unexplained or unaccounted for phenomena, or disturbing elements that might have influenced the results. It was noted that hypotheses often are accepted with qualifications.[4] Cautions for using conclusions that bear qualifications should be given here. Even though the investigator has exerted special care not to generalize either his conclusions or recommendations beyond the scope of the study, the reader might, if not given a caveat here.

One should be honest, with no attempt made to cover up shortcomings or offer excuses. A perfectly errorless study is difficult to achieve. Apologetic attitudes are not in order, neither are "hedge words," which

4. Cf., p. 34.

minimize the importance or magnitude of an error.[5] Researchers are only human: they make mistakes. Good researchers reduce their errors to a minimum; poor researchers can not hide shoddy work from astute readers. A dislike of confessing shortcomings is human nature, but when it is realized that acknowledging error can improve subsequent efforts, it is less discomforting.

5. Cf., p. 52.

Chapter 7

Reference Section

All information that can illustrate, amplify, or verify data presented in the main text, but would have cluttered up the body of the thesis, is gathered together for inclusion in the Reference Section, which consists of Appendixes and a Bibliography. Depending upon stylistic preferences, their order can be reversed.

Appendixes

Material relegated to Appendixes is important or useful, but not essential to understanding the thesis. This includes material that can amplify or illustrate the text, but whose length, detail, or format detracts from communicating with the desired clarity and directness. Appendixes can also furnish supportive or factual information that helps validate portions of the data.

Each appendix should have a specific reference made to it at least once during the main text. Information not relevant enough to be worth mentioning does not belong in the thesis. Materials that are appropriate for appendixes include:

data-gathering devices (e.g., questionnaires, interview blanks, form letters, tests, forms, schedules);

illustrative materials (e.g., photographs, documents, musical examples);

copies of documents not ordinarily available or readily accessible to the reader;

lists of sources of information (e.g., school systems, individuals);

statistical calculations;

lengthy tables from which summary tables were derived for the main text;

tables presenting data of minor importance (as distinguished from those presenting major data in the text);

lengthy quotations;

legal decisions, laws, or other legal documents;

technical notes;

original data.

On occasion one might wish to detail or illustrate a suggested course of action which stems from a Recommendation (q.v.) and is based upon findings reported in the text. An appendix is the proper place to include such a proposal.

Bibliography

Strictly speaking, a bibliography is a list of writings related to the problem investigated. Common usage admits other sources that are not actually bibliographic; e.g., personal interviews, speeches, recordings. Thus, a bibliography in a thesis is a general list of all sources pertinent to the problem which were consulted during the research. Descriptive details are furnished that identify each source accurately, including its origin, date, and form. Bibliographies help other researchers construct their own working bibliographies.

Obviously, one can not list all sources which relate in a general way to the study, unless the problem area is extremely limited. A bibliography's purpose in a thesis is to provide a *useful* list from which all deadwood has been culled. Contrary to what some neophytes evidently think, padded lists do not impress knowledgeable readers because of their length. Such lists are not only scholastically dishonest, but can mislead other researchers.

The bibliography is one important measure of the strength of scholarship revealed by the thesis. Experienced readers censure inflated lists, inclusion of sources not distinctively helpful, materials of questionable validity, or omission of sources known to be basic to the problem area. A carefully selected bibliography of reliable sources is scholastically strongest and most helpful to other researchers.

Two criticisms of bibliographies can be singled out for comment here, because they occur so frequently. One is that all items cited in footnote entries do not appear. Carefully checking every footnote against the bibliography will insure this does not happen. The second fault is that recent items have not been consulted. One way to evaluate a thesis quickly is to glance at the dates for all items in the bibliography as a test for recency of data. Of course, many older sources (particularly, primary sources or definitive works) are perfectly valid; however, an investigator is expected to base his findings upon the latest available data (including the most recent editions of books). Outdated evidence creates doubts about the merits of the entire study.

Occasionally, a bibliography may be annotated to increase its value to other researchers. When extensive or diversified lists are used, which is typical of graduate theses, the materials can be organized into categories; e.g., "Books," "Articles," "Unpublished Materials," "Government Documents," "Personal Interviews." A diverse assortment of only a few items can be grouped under the caption "Other Materials," or "Miscellany."

Chapter 8

General Considerations

Good writers in any genre adapt to their readers. Researchers, who *inform* a limited circle of knowledgeable and critical colleagues, write on a scholarly level.

Put quite simply, scholarly writing reflects scholarly thought. Scholarly thought is logical, factual, objective. Scholars discard all that is superfluous or abtruse in their craving to arrive at unadorned truths. They base original thought upon objective examination of accurate evidence. They communicate in precise terms. Scholarly writers present ideas in an organized, logical arrangement, take care to be objective, draw interpretations from fact, and use exact, clear language.

Inexperienced writers too often think scholarly writing is a verbal costume or affectation they must don, rather than a genuine expression of the kind of intellect that governed their research. They self-consciously write to *impress* their peers with their erudition and depth of thought, forgetting that their purpose is to *inform* in explicit terms. As a result, they frequently produce bloated language and ponderous syntax. True scholarly writing, on the other hand, is exemplified when complex ideas are presented in lucid prose. A writer ought to strive for an inverse relationship: the more profound the thought, the simpler its expression.

Bearing in mind always that their purpose is to inform, good research writers give first consideration to content. How to achieve worthwhile content (i.e., what is entailed in sound research) is not this handbook's concern. Fledgling writers can be alerted, nonetheless, to two cautions about reporting content. First, every important fact or idea must be recorded. If all relevant material is included in first drafts, the report can be condensed later to only that information essential to understanding the study.[1] Then, the investigator must be prepared to defend every statement he makes in his thesis.[2]

The second consideration must be for organization. Ideas can not be thrown at a reader willy-nilly. They must be sorted, arranged, and properly

1. Cf., Brevity, p. 58.
2. Cf., Documentation, p. 44.

related. A disorganized thesis can so exasperate a reader that he will put it aside unfinished. Content is made intelligible through logical organization.

The third consideration is for the mode of expression; in other words, *style.* Many a dull thesis is acceptable in matters of content, organization, and sophisticated command of written language. Effective style transcends these elements. With a little coaching—and a lot of revision—even inexperienced writers can lift their theses above the level of pedantry and tedium.

Entire books are available that can help improve one's written communication. The subject is too broad to be treated in one chapter of a handbook; nevertheless, certain observations can be made that will assist a writer to adhere to the conventions of scholarly writing without gravitating into idiomatic weaknesses. By following the suggestions given in this chapter, one can develop a feeling for writing effective professional literature.

Documentation

Researchers should always write with the specter of critics standing at their shoulders to challenge the validity of each sentence. Only when every statement can be substantiated can it be hoped that a thesis will pass examination.

Once young scholars accept this proposition, they understandably become confused about how much documentation is required, beyond that given to direct quotations or paraphrased words of others. Should every sentence bear a footnote citation to establish authority? Those familiar with reporting research know this is not necessary, but inexperienced reporters need guidance. Overdocumentation is undesirable. Copious footnotes not only interrupt the main ideas being developed and detract psychologically from the presentation, but lead the reader to suspect he is being given a recitation of facts that have not been synthesized into the writer's thoughts. Underdocumentation substantially weakens a study due to doubts raised in the reader's mind about the data's validity.

The answer to the dilemma of documentation is simple. Only three kinds of statements may be admitted into theses: facts, opinions, and basic assumptions. Certain facts and all opinions require documentation.

Some facts are widely known, easily verified. No one will challenge seriously that Herbert Hoover was President of the United States, or that the Detroit Tigers belong to the American League in professional baseball. Information like that can be confirmed easily in several readily available sources, or is common knowledge. It needs no documentation.

Other facts are commonly known within an academic discipline. A statement that a Baroque organ differs in constructional details from a Romantic organ will not be argued among musicians. Enologists recognize that, of thirty-two species of grapes, only *vitis vinifer* produces great wines. Facts that appear throughout the literature for a discipline ordinarily require no documentation. As long as one or more items in his Bibliography (q.v.) contain the information, the student has authority to which he can refer should questions arise.

Still other facts do require documentation. These facts are

not well known, even with a discipline;

contradictory to other facts or suppositions;

obscure, or difficult for the reader to verify;

specific pieces of information that bear directly upon important points;

brought in from other disciplines;

in some way open to question, because readers are not as well-informed about the problem as the researcher.[3]

The kinds of facts described above are uncovered and brought to the investigation. In this sense they do not originate from the study. Original facts, i.e., those that emerge from data gathered during the investigation, have no validity other than that of the data itself. They can not be referred to authority. Verification is accomplished by providing the necessary explanations about how data were derived, confirmed, and analyzed.[4]

New information, formed when the investigator synthesizes existing facts, obviously can not be documented, because it has not existed before. It stands inquiry on the basis of reason. Facts that come out of interpretations of the findings fall into this category. As an example, here is the derivation of a "new" fact.

1. *Fact:* Two cubes are of the same dimensions.

2. *Fact:* One cube is of iron, the other of aluminum.

3. *Finding:* The iron cube weighs more than the aluminum.

4. *New Fact:* Iron is heavier than aluminum per unit of bulk.

Opinions carry little weight in the quest for truth when measured against facts. Nevertheless, there are instances in which no evidence can be found except for expert opinion. Whenever expert opinion is presented in a thesis,

3. Cf., the caution about assuming the reader knows more than he does, first given on pp. 15-16.
4. Cf., p. 29.

it should be clearly identified (e.g., "White believed . . .," or, "In White's opinion . . .") and given proper documentation. Opinions, such as those taken from an opinionnaire, which make up raw data for a study, bear the intrinsic validity of data.

An investigator's personal opinion should not appear. The author impresses upon his students that they are not expert enough to have an informed opinion until *after* their studies are accepted—an admonition that also helps guard against bias creeping into their statements. If, for some reason, an investigator feels compelled to express an opinion, it should be placed as a footnote commentary and labeled clearly.

Basic assumptions have been discussed earlier.[5] A researcher is not expected to document his basic assumptions, except in those instances wherein specific reference is made to the particular research upon which an assumption has been based.

Organization of the Thesis[6]

Theses can not communicate information clearly and concisely without being properly organized. Preceding chapters have developed an organizational scheme for main divisions. Although this scheme is neither arbitrary nor inflexible, it does approach standardization because it is dictated by the inner logic of scholarship. Simply placing material into this design is not enough, however. Good writers extend principles of organization to their basic units of thought—individual sentences.

Tests for Organization

Effective organization is an outgrowth of sound logic and proper emphasis. Scrupulous writers can apply four tests for organization to their manuscripts, starting with sentences, then moving progressively through larger divisions:

1. Does its (sentence, paragraph, section, chapter) internal arrangement express a connected idea?

2. Do its parts relate so as to make its meaning perfectly clear?

3. Do its most important elements receive emphasis, with the others subordinated?

4. Does its appearance at this point in the thesis make it more effective than at any other point?

5. Cf., p. 22.
6. Cf., Organization of the Data, p. 31.

The first two deal with internal logic, the third with internal emphasis, the fourth with external logic and emphasis. Writers who challenge their work with these tests will find themselves rewriting sentences; rearranging sentences within paragraphs or moving them into other paragraphs; reshuffling paragraphs or transplanting them into other sections; or, reordering entire sections.

Outlining

No other technique is as helpful in organizing a thesis than outlining. Outlining forces a writer to clarify his ideas. When ideas are set down in skeletal fashion, gaps in thought, faulty relationships, digressions, needless repetition, discontinuities, and needs for effective transitions become more obvious. It is easier to remedy weaknesses by rearranging, grouping, and relating seminal ideas before they are expanded into finished prose, which obscures organization and psychologically becomes inflexible.

Whenever a writer experiences difficulty in organizing any portion of his thesis, he can attack the problem by moving ideas into new and different arrangements, which is done easily with an outline. Experimenting in this way is recommended regardless of whether one perceives problems with organization. Looking at fresh relationships prevents becoming "locked in" to the first way in which thoughts occur or are written down.

The outline should be refined continually throughout the writing period. Periodically, the outline for the Presentation, Analysis, and Interpretation of Data (q.v.) should be reviewed to insure that it organizes the evidence to test the Statement of the Hypothesis (q.v.).

Controlling Emphasis

Outlining is useful, too, for positioning ideas, an easy and useful technique for controlling emphasis. Main ideas are placed in positions of strongest emphasis—at beginnings and endings. With directness of communication an attribute, placing main ideas first is favored in smaller units—sentences and paragraphs. Placing topic sentences at the beginning of paragraphs provides an additional benefit for readers: they can skim through portions of the thesis by reading topic sentences, passing quickly through material already familiar, or refreshing themselves quickly with previously read text.

At times a writer will find building to the main point effective, placing it last for emphasis. An idea that takes several paragraphs to develop lends itself naturally to this procedure. Sections of theses often state important ideas last, pulling them from the middle, or developmental, part of the discussion. The psychology of stating the whole idea first, developing it in its details, then restating it at the last is useful in theses, which treat complicated and involved ideas.

Psychologically, a greater amount of space given to a thought suggests greater importance; consequently, subordinate ideas should take less space than main ones. Correction of any imbalance should not be made by inflating primary ideas, if they are already adequately stated, but by reducing space for the secondary. This often can be accomplished by relegating material to Appendixes (q.v.).

Constructional techniques can also be employed for emphasis. Parallel construction is one. Consecutive sentences or phrases that begin with the same grammatical construction reinforce the statements of closely related and nondisparite ideas. Contrast is another constructional technique. For example, a short sentence following a series of longer sentences can stress an important idea. A short paragraph following a series of longer paragraphs can achieve the same purpose.

Devices of Format (q.v.) help provide emphasis. Wide margins around important ideas make them stand out, as when they are placed in indented lists. Capital letters or italics (underlining) can be used, although if not used judiciously they soon lose their effectiveness. Numbering calls attention to a succession of related thoughts. Dashes set off important ideas within sentences. The use of headings is an important technique for creating emphasis.

Self-sufficient Sections

An important consideration for organization. but one frequently overlooked by inexperienced writers, is that theses are read *discontinuously*. Those who read them are professional people, who have busy schedules and competing demands for their attention that cause interruptions. The time intervening before they can resume reading can be lengthy. Aside from that, one should pause occasionally to relax from weighty and often detailed material. Assimilating the contents of an entire thesis at one sitting can be mentally exhausting. A thesis made up of sections which are more or less self-sufficient in the ideas each presents facilitates reading on an interrupted schedule. Descriptive headings, a product of sectionalization, make it easier to follow the discussion.

Many writers open chapters (other than the first and last) with a short statement telling what will be found, and end them with a brief statement of what was covered, including how the chapter contributed to the entire study. These statements make it easier for a reader to follow the ideas developed in each chapter and to regain the train of thought upon returning to the thesis.[7] Such previews and summaries are not needless repetition, if they contain key ideas and eschew details.

---

7. This practice is recommended by the author. It also makes the final Summary (q.v.) easier to write. The longer the thesis, the more important chapter summaries become.

Vocabulary

An effective vocabulary, the most obvious hallmark of any good writing style, exhibits words that are

well-suited to the purposes of the text,

keyed to the anticipated audience's comprehension level, and

fitted naturally into the writer's personal idiom.

Choosing words with these qualifications that blend nicely into scholarly style requires untiring effort. While the best writers seem to display an instinct for the "right" word, more often than not their "knack" represents hours spent sorting through alternatives to arrive at the best choices.

Research reporters, whose purpose it is to transmit information efficiently, should choose words because they convey meanings clearly and without equivocation, not for their length or their impressiveness, although long or learned-sounding words certainly are not ruled out. An erroneous notion seems to exist in some circles that an inflated vocabulary, per se, equates with scholarship. On the contrary, an ornate vocabulary can obscure, rather than enhance, explicit communication between writer and reader.

Addressing a report to other scholars permits a writer to use a sophisticated vocabulary without losing his readers; yet, a sophisticated vocabulary possesses inherent dangers. One can slip easily into pedantry through overuse of heavy language. Highly specialized or obscure technical language can obstruct communication with all but a select group of "insiders," even within the same discipline. There is no reason, say, for microbiologists not to be able to speak to macrobiologists.

Writers who become self-conscious about addressing their peers are tempted to sprinkle impressive words throughout their theses indiscriminately, or to manufacture excuses for inserting them. The usual results are awkward expression, uneven style, and obvious pretension. Students are encouraged to expand their vocabularies judiciously, of course—dictionaries and thesaruses are valuable tools for this purpose, as long as they are used to search out the "right" word, not merely to find longer words or rarer synonyms—but style quickly degenerates into psuedoscholarship when words are selected only to impress.[8] Discriminately selected learned-sounding words will slip unaffectedly into a writer's prose when

8. Synonyms rarely have exactly the same meanings. Using terms interchangeably runs the risk of confusing the reader.

their meanings are completely understood in the contexts in which they are employed;

they fit comfortably into the scholar's vocabulary (he does not stumble over them or feel awkward when reading them aloud); and,

they express ideas more accurately, more effectively, or more succinctly than the words they supplant.

Precise Meanings

Above all, words must be precise. Ideas can not be transmitted accurately in language which is equivocal. This is especially true when communication is one-directional, with no feedback to indicate how well the reader understands, no opportunity to elaborate, explain, or correct. Even experienced writers frequently are surprised to find that "perfectly clear" statements have been interpreted differently from what they intended. Using words with precise meanings that are agreed upon by both writer and reader is the only way explicit communication can be accomplished.

The criterion of precision automatically discards many words used in other modes of expression: the dynamics of a living language create problems with the words that remain. One persistent problem is that words carry connotative meanings. Connotative meanings can not be used in scholarly writing, because they lack objectivity (i.e., they show emotion or suggest bias), and are not known to or agreed upon by all readers. Words with connotations strong enough to endanger their denotations are to be treated with caution.

Dealing with only precise denotative meanings is not easy. Meanings change through the years. Words acquire new definitions; meanings sometimes fade and become obsolescent. Each new edition of a dictionary testifies to these phenomena. Meanings also change when words are used in different contexts, as different parts of speech, or with different groups of people. Compiling lists of meanings for randomly selected words as they are used in all forms of expression (including technical, colloquial, slang) is an entertaining exercise that quickly dramatizes to writers how easily their statements can be misconstrued (does, "The subject did not feel like continuing . . .," mean the subject physically was not up to it, or mentally did not care to?). The widespread use of double-entendre in humor is another illustration of how words hold more than one meaning.

Dictionaries are the final arbiters, the only acceptable sources of agreement on meanings between writer and reader, aside from the Definition of Terms (q.v.). A standard dictionary should be within easy reach whenever a writer works on his thesis, "to be used," as Barzun and Graff astutely put it, *"more often* than is necessary. . . ."[9] Only modern meanings are used, except in special circumstances that are made known to the reader. When several definitions are given for a word, the meaning intended must be self-evident within the context of the passage. Definitions labeled as dialectal, slang, or in other ways not part of the standard vocabulary of English, are ruled out. Standard English is used to report research, because it is substantially uniform, and well established in usage by educated people.

Indefinite Meanings

Words or phrases that do not say what they mean, or do not mean what they say, are used so frequently in ordinary communication that they infiltrate theses, unless students are constantly on guard. *Descriptive adjectives* and *adverbs of manner or degree* are leading offenders. An alert writer can spot those that enliven and intensify literary prose by their dramatic or emotional overtones (e.g., "colossal," "shocking," "excruciatingly," "epic," "magnificent," "superbly"). The more subdued, like those in this list, can slip past writers who do not treat *all* modifiers with caution.

almost	most(ly)
appreciable(bly)	much
approximate(ly)	near(ly)
bad(ly)	negligible(bly)
beautiful(ly)	nice(ly)
comparative(ly)	relative(ly)
considerable(bly)	several
effective(ly)	significant(ly)
excessive(ly)	similar(ly)
fair(ly)	sizeable
far	small
few	some(what)
good	sufficient(ly)
great(ly)	suitable(bly)
important(ly)	tall
large(ly)	unusual(ly)
less	valuable
many	very
more	well

9. Jacques Barzun and Henry F. Graff, *The Modern Researcher* (New York: Harcourt, Brace and Co., 1957), p. 251.

51

Abstract nouns—nouns that name attributes or qualities—obscure the meanings of sentences in which they are found. Their abstractness is compounded when they are coupled with meaningless modifiers. Nouns like those in the following list need concrete modifiers, accompanying illustrations, or further explanations to give them determinate content.

art	intelligence
beauty	love
character	majority
composition	magnitude
condition	meaning
conservative	need
emotion	radical
enjoyment	significance
feeling	society
form	tendency
importance	value

Hedge words and phrases, which avoid making positive or forthright statements, make up a special category of vague meanings. Scholars are prone to employ hedging tactics, because they are understandably loath to make dogmatic statements—they wish to remain open-minded. There is also a tendency to lapse into hedging terms when reporting negative results. Common hedge terms include:

appears to	possibly
as far as is known	probably
attempt has been made	rather
certain aspects	reasonably
generally	seems to
evidently	selected factors
in the usual way	should (conditional)
may	some factors
might	tends to
more or less	to some degree
nearly	various
perhaps	well under (over)

Euphemisms are another category of terms that do not say what they mean. Euphemisms are mild or inoffensive expressions that are substituted for unpleasant or offensive words, because the writer does not wish to offend. Society's vocabulary is replete with euphemisms like these:

disadvantaged	passed away
exceptional child	senior citizen
golden years	social disease
handicapped person	underprivileged

Other imprecise words and expressions, with reasons for not using them, are:

Figures of Speech—used for the sake of effect.

Jargon—outlandish or hybrid language; highly specialized technical terminology; or obscure and pretentious language.

Vogue Words—a kind of jargon, typified by bureaucratic gobbledegook, which overworks otherwise serviceable words like "viable," or "awesome," and is especially fond of adding the suffixes "wise" and "ize" to standard terms ("budgetwise," "utopianize").

Cliches—trite and hackneyed expressions.

Slang and Vulgarisms—substandard and coarse.

Absolute Meanings

Absolute terms suggest dogmatism, bias, closemindedness, and exaggerated self-assurance. They should rarely appear in theses. Examples are:

absolutely	never
always	perfectly
invariably	nothing has been written
it is necessary	should (mandatory)
must	

Spelling

Spellings must be correct and orthodox. Shortened spellings like *nite,* or *thru,* do not belong in scholarly writing. The advice to use the dictionary *more often* than is necessary for meanings applies equally to spellings.[10] Whenever there is a choice between two accepted spellings, the first spelling

---

10. Cf., pp. 50-51. Dictionaries also indicate the division points at which words may be broken at the ends of lines.

given in a good American dictionary is recommended.[11] For example, both *aesthetic* and *esthetic* are accepted spellings. *Esthetic* is listed as a variation of *aesthetic;* therefore, *aesthetic* is preferred. *Acknowledgment* is listed also as *acknowledgement.* The first spelling is preferred.

Whatever form is decided upon, spellings must remain consistent. *Analogue* in one part of the thesis should not become *analog* in another. Spelling rules do not apply to quotations, which are copied exactly as found in their original forms.[12]

Grammar

The rules of grammar are abused in so much of what is read and heard daily that one must be vigilant lest this assault on intelligibility taint his writing style. Although some might argue that new usages are permissable changes in a living language, there is one incontrovertible reason for adhering to established rules; viz., *that is the only way to be absolutely clear in statement.* Every writer should keep a handbook of English grammar near his typewriter.

Improper linkage of modifiers with the words they modify, and faulty relationships of pronouns with their antecedents are probably the most prevalent grammatical errors found in theses. All modifiers—words, phrases, clauses—should be positioned as closely as possible to the words they change the meanings of. Two sentences illustrate what occurs when they are not (modifiers, and terms they should modify, are in italics).

Although precipitated by the coagulent, the test proved the *chemical* could be used as a diluent.

Subject A *revealed* that he had used an alias *during the interview.*

In the first example, the meaning can be inferred from the context of the sentence, although a reader should not have to hesitate to be sure of relationships. In the second, careless placement links the modifying phrase to the wrong verb and changes the meaning.

Participles are especially troublesome when it comes to proper linkage. Present participles, in particular, have an uncanny way of being left dangling, with no word to modify, as illustrated in the next examples.

After adjusting the valve, the engine [?] performed without a malfunction.

---

11. The latest edition of *Webster's New Collegiate Dictionary* is recommended.
12. Writers are reminded to consult their style manuals on the use of *sic.*

Discounting the effects of inflation, a bushel of wheat [?] brings a farmer less money than five years ago.

The words the participles seem to link with obviously do not perform the action. Every word ending in *ing* should automatically be examined to see if it is a present participle. If it is, a link with a noun or noun equivalent must be found. The safest practice is to use participles sparingly, especially in present tense.[13]

Contemporary jargonese makes heavy use of attributive nouns—nouns used as adjective equivalents and placed before other nouns—frequently with an attendant loss in clarity. This title, e.g., raises questions:

Title: Gulf Coast Sea Nettle and Jellyfish Infestation

Questions: Are these species of sea nettles and jellyfish that are found only along the Gulf Coast?
Is the Gulf Coast infested by sea nettles and jellyfish, or are these particular species infesting another region?
Are sea nettles and jellyfish along the Gulf Coast being infested?
Are "Gulf Coast" sea nettles, along with jellyfish, being infested (or are they infesting another region)?

When two or more nouns modify another noun, pains must be taken that meanings remain clear.

Improper, or "fuzzy" relationships are found frequently between pronouns and their antecedents. *Every* pronoun should be checked to see if

it refers to the right antecedent;

its antecedent is immediately evident (a reader must not have to search for an antecedent);

it agrees with its antecedent in gender, person, number, and case.

Many statements can be strengthened by replacing pronouns with their antecedents. The following statement becomes much clearer when the antecedent in the first sentence (in italics) replaces the italicized pronoun in the second.

Scholars must be careful with *pronouns* in their theses. This caution is given because frequently *they* have faulty relationships with their antecedents.

13. Past participles suggest Passive Voice (q.v.), which is overused in theses.

Punctuation

Careful punctuation clarifies written expression; slipshod punctuation can alter meanings. English handbooks, dictionaries, and style manuals will answer general questions about punctuation, but there are no hard and fast rules. Writers can check their punctuation by asking, "Will a reader be able to interpret this sentence *only* as I intended it?". In this connection, graduate students probably have most trouble with the omission of commas that should be used to subordinate material (as in nonrestrictive clauses), and to set off the last item in a series (a comma should be placed before the conjuction preceding the last item). A reader can not be expected to subordinate and differentiate correctly in unfamiliar text. For example, an investigator who writes this,

> The current flowing through the yellow wire activated the relay which set off lights in the red and black, yellow and green, orange and blue panels.

can not mean this,

> The current, flowing through the yellow wire, activated the relay, which set off lights in the red and black, yellow and green, orange, and blue panels.

Person

Theses should be written in third person. Writers new to scholarly style usually must undergo an adjustment period before feeling comfortable with this convention. Elimination of first and second person (along with the editorial "we") not only conveys the calm restraint and objectivity that should characterize research, but protects the discourse from becoming informal, "chatty," and careless.

Tense

A thesis describes events that have already happened; hence, it is written in past tense. Whenever a verb is found in present or future tense, the sentence should be examined to see whether past tense is not correct.

Present tense can be permitted for timeless truths—"Moliere *is* the author of . . .," "Hydrogen and oxygen *combine* to form . . .," "The Declaration of Independence *states*. . . ." Future tense may be used on infrequent occasions when referring within the thesis itself— "Information relative to . . . *will be found* in Table VI," or, "This analysis of variance technique *will be explained* in Chapter IV." For most purposes, exclusive use of past tense is the safest practice.[14]

Voice

Formal style, stressing impersonality, fosters excessive use of passive voice. Passive voice is indirect, vague, and wordy. It is indirect because the subject of the verb is acted upon; the actor is removed or obscured.[15]

The substance was found to have been contaminated.

The reading had been taken by the laboratory assistant after the temperature drop.

Referring to actors obliquely clouds expression. Passive voice creates wordiness because it always requires a verb phrase, rather than a verb, and leads to roundabout ways of stating thoughts. A reader should not need to hesitate or wade through unnecessarily long phrases to be certain of a meaning. To overcome the indirect tone created by passive voice, actors can be reinstated, if they are not already present, and the order of action reversed. In active voice subjects act, verbs express actions, and objects receive actions. Changes to active voice can be made without foregoing impersonality or pervasive past tense.

Passive Voice: It was announced that the project had been approved.
It was announced by the committee [actor inserted] that the project had been approved.

Active Voice: The committee announced that the project had been approved.

From a stylistic standpoint, excessive use of passive voice makes for a dull presentation; yet, this is a prevalent weakness in scholarly writing. Every attempt should be made to use active voice, unless the actor is ob-

14. The author favors past tense for introducing quotations, although this is not widely practiced. "Giles *said* . . .," or, "Giles *stated* in 1956 . . . ," is preferred over "Giles *says* . . . ," because Giles obviously stated whatever he had to say prior to the time it is quoted. Besides, Giles should he accorded the privilege of changing his opinion. In any event, past tense, dated by the reference source, does not commit Giles to the same opinion at later dates or under different circumstances. If the person cited is deceased, there is reason to argue that the quotation falls under "timeless truths," making present tense acceptable.

15. One reason bureaucratic correspondence is rife with passive voice is that, by removing the actor, responsibility is avoided. "I" did not decide, "It was decided."

vious, unknown, or unimportant, or the object should be stressed (e.g., "He was hit," "The goal was reached").

Brevity

Good scholars come directly to the point, disclosing their information in a minimum of words. With the flood of reading matter published in every field, economy of expression is seen as a virtue by those who try to remain current with their professional literature.

Brevity must not be interpreted as laconicism. Short, choppy sentences make for poor style and disjointed thought. Neither should brevity become understatement or abridgment. Brevity means stating only what the occasion requires—not less, but no more.

"To be brief, first be long" is a good maxim. Placing all relevant information on paper during initial drafts guards against omitting any important ideas, no matter how verbosely they might be stated. Preoccupation with screening content or eliminating wordiness can interrupt thought flow during the "white heat" of inspiration. One can too easily get halted on a decision about whether to include an idea, a search for the "right" word, or an attempt to purify a sentence. Subsequent revisions will remove what can go without endangering understanding. Admittedly, deleting something once it is written is difficult psychologically; however, omitting essential content is more serious than including the insignificant. Effective writers discipline themselves to excise unimportant material.

A manuscript's length can be reduced in two ways, as suggested in the preceding paragraph. The first way is to prune content to only that information deemed necessary for the reader's understanding. Many passages—including some the writer will count among his best efforts—will be struck when the question is asked, "Will the thesis suffer if this statement is deleted?" An outline is valuable for identifying material that is unessential, or for pointing out where needless repetition can be eliminated.[16] Content in the main text can be reduced further by following suggestions given for shortening Quotations (q.v.), and by removing everything that can go into Appendixes (q.v.). Most pruning of content will be done during the first readings for Revision (q.v.).

Once content has been settled upon, individual sentences can be reworked to eliminate verbiage. Each sentence, each clause, can be mentally reduced to its subject, predicate, and object, then reassembled with superfluous words removed.

16. Cf., p. 47.

Unnecessary or vague modifiers can be eliminated.

will have no separate categories at all (will have no separate categories)
was wholly eliminated (was eliminated)
truly notable growth (notable growth)

Phrases and clauses can be reduced to fewer words. Verb phrases that end with prepositions, and constructions that begin with "it" or "if" and end with "that" usually signal opportunities to reduce words.

writers in the modern age (modern writers)
the responsibilities of each of the program areas (each program area's responsibilities)
made a study of (studied)
was found in agreement with (agreed)
it was apparent that (obviously)
if circumstances arise that (should)

Tautologies—needless repetition of the same meaning in different words—should be removed.

most, but not all (most)
round in shape (round)
plan ahead (plan)

Articles can be eliminated. Most writers overuse "the." Articles can be dropped by changing singular subjects to plural, without losing the sense of the sentence.

The proponents of (Proponents of)
In active voice a subject acts, a verb expresses the action, and an object receives the action. (In active voice subjects act, verbs express actions, and objects receive actions.)

Circumlocutions can be streamlined. Roundabout ways of stating thoughts are clarified and shortened by placing important ideas in main clauses, and placing main clauses in positions of importance (first or last).

It was necessary, of course, that, in the interim between the inception of the study and the conclusion of the data-collection, measures be taken to insure the anonymity of the investigator. (The investigator had to remain anonymous until all data were in.)

Some deleted words may be reinstated when the manuscript is revised for readability, because telegraphic delivery is not desirable, except when used occasionally for emphasis;[17] nevertheless, reworking sentences for brevity discards verbiage, with a resultant improvement in clarity and directness of communication.

Revision

A refined, polished thesis reflects credit upon the student, the department he represents, and the academic discipline. Praiseworthy efforts are possible, even by first-time writers, provided they are willing to revise, revise, revise.

Graduate students sometimes become upset over the neverending changes their professors suggest. Nothing satisfies, they complain. The professor edits what he himself had previously rewritten. His latest revision reverted to an earlier version. These changes are not made because professors refuse to be pleased, or are capricious in their expectations. On the contrary, professors are obligated to help their students produce the best theses possible. They owe their students whatever lessons in editing they can give.

Learning to rework a manuscript constitutes one more important step toward a scholar's independence. Self-criticism, dissatisfaction with anything but the best expression, constant polishing, mark good writers in any style. Written words are not immutable, although they tend to remain fixed, once put on paper. Good writers search for alternative ways of expressing their thoughts. Each time a sentence is reread the scholar should ask, "How can I say this differently," "How can this be improved?". Then he must expect that *any* change—even in one word—can cause revisions in adjoining sentences, in nearby paragraphs, often in other parts of the thesis.

Although rewriting usually takes place during initial drafts, portions of a thesis ordinarily are completed individually, not necessarily in sequence, and over a relatively long period. As a result, character and tone can be inconsistent, thought disjointed, and emphases misplaced. A thesis benefits from revisions that consider it *in toto*.

Final revisions are more effective when made after the writer has put the manuscript aside for a time. It is surprising how mannerisms, monotony of sentence construction, and other stylistic weaknesses stand out upon returning to the work. Sentences that pleased when they were written will appear awkward or not in character. Ideas that seemed to be stated explicitly will be seen to have other interpretations. Emphases will need readjustment. Unfortunately, practical considerations of time schedules and deadlines usually preclude adequate time for respite from writing; still, the amount of im-

17. Cf., p. 61.

60

provement that can be made with only a few days rest is proportionately so great in terms of time that one should make every effort to build recesses into his writing schedule.[18]

A suggested plan for revision is to read the thesis for content first, to assure that the information is adequate and accurate. During these readings, a writer can use his outline to check for organization and emphasis.[19] Techniques for reducing content described under Brevity (q.v.) can be used to shorten the manuscript.

When satisfied that content is satisfactory and organization effective, the writer can revise his statements to improve clarity, utilizing ideas discussed in sections dealing with Organization (q.v.), Vocabulary (q.v.), Grammar (q.v.), Punctuation (q.v.), and Brevity (q.v.). All statements must be explicit, with no chance for alternative interpretations, with nothing left to inference. Clear writing means more than stating ideas that can be understood; ideas must be written so they can not be *mis*understood.

Finally, revisions can be made to bring variety to the manuscript. The writing can be enlivened through variety in

choice of words,

lengths of words,

lengths of sentences,

lengths of paragraphs,

sentence construction (especially, so they do not all begin the same way).

Revision for variety is part of improving readability. Inexperienced writers easily fall into the monotony of setting down ideas one after the other without a sense of good prose. A thesis should read smoothly, with connections and transitions between paragraphs. Spoken style is more natural, more idiomatic than written expression; consequently, theses can be improved in readability by reading them aloud. Sometimes the ear will detect what the eye does not:

unnecessary words,

awkward phraseology,

unintentional repetition,

needs for transitional clauses or sentences.

18. Cf., Time Considerations, p. 64.
19. Cf., Outlining, p. 47.

The suggestion to read aloud does not mean that the writer should use his ear as authority for grammar, nor does it mean that one should write the way he talks. The purpose of reading aloud is to infuse written expression with the natural rhythm, euphony, and cadence of spoken expression.

Format

A thesis manuscript is given a final polish by examining its format. This inspection does more than cover matters of physical form that are dictated by the style manual and are followed while typing the final copy. It is a check on internal matters that affect style. A glance through the manuscript will reveal whether enough headings are used to speed the reader through the text.[20] The writer can detect if an overuse of footnotes detracts psychologically from the presentation, or if frequent or long quotations create the same adverse effect.[21] By leafing through the manuscript, the writer can see whether italics (underlining), capital letters, dashes, inset lists, or other devices set off important ideas, and, if so, whether they are used judiciously.[22]

Paragraphs can be checked to see if they vary in length—a clue to variety in expression. Too many short paragraphs indicate that the text is choppy, rough, and irregular, the ideas presented starkly, without being transformed into graceful prose. One sentence paragraphs should occur rarely, if at all. They are strong indications that ideas have not been expanded into thoughtful discourse. On the other extreme, too many long paragraphs indicate a dull, flat presentation. As a general rule, paragraphs should not be over one typewritten page in length—never over five hundred words.

Less obvious at a glance than lengths of paragraphs, but equally important for style are the lengths of sentences. Sentences should not fall into a monotonous sameness. Neither short nor long sentences should predominate.[23] Short sentences or paragraphs can be combined, and long sentences or paragraphs broken up to add variety, as long as the combination or dissolution is accomplished in accordance with the dictates of correct grammar, accurate punctuation, and good sentence or paragraph sense.

---

20. Cf., p. 48.

21. Cf., p. 30 and 44.

22. Cf., p. 48.

23. As a general guide, sentences and paragraphs can be kept short to assist the reader through complex and difficult to grasp ideas, and lengthened for less complex, more readily understood thoughts.

Proofreading

Before the final draft is taken to the typist, it should be correct in every detail. Many students pay an English graduate student or teacher to edit their work. Nothing is wrong with submitting copy to someone more expert in matters of English usage; however, certain precautions must be observed. For one, scholarly vocabulary, expression, and punctuation are more precise than literary or accepted common practice. A person who edits scholarly papers should be familiar with scholarly modes of writing. Secondly, the editing will not be done for content. Words that have been typed correctly, but inadvertently substituted for similar words, or technical terms used incorrectly might pass undetected. "Grade school," e.g., might pass a reader's inspection, when "graduate school" was intended. "Recession" can slip by for "recision."

Every detail of the final draft must be clear to the typist. Corrections and insertions should be marked plainly, so they make their way properly into the final copy. Involved marginal notations can be confused, oral instructions forgotten. A typist's duty is to transform the draft into clean typescript in good mechanical form. She is not to exercise editorial license.

If the typist is not familiar with the style manual to be followed, all necessary instructions should be given clearly. A typist who types many papers for students of one university, school, or department can be more familiar with the style manual than the writer of the thesis. Some students find it worth a few cents a page extra in typing fees for the typist to perform the additional chore of correcting faulty form; however, it is the student's responsibility to familiarize himself thoroughly with the style manual. This is accomplished by the simple expedient of using the style manual consistently from the first paper written in one's graduate studies. Matters of form then become routine.

When the copy returns from the typist, the writer should assure himself first that it follows the form prescribed by the style manual. Then it is given an exacting proofreading, *which compares it with the final draft.* This should be done in several short sittings. It is difficult, at best, to find all errors, particularly in one's own work. To read too much at one sitting leads to boredom and fatigue, and mitigates against meticulous proofreading, especially when one knows what is said (or what was intended to be said) before reading the copy. Because proofreading one's own words is always risky, someone else's services are recommended for a final proofreading.

Corrections should be made before the thesis is placed in the hands of ths examining committee. Despite all care taken in proofreading, it is unusual if the committee does not find errors, or does not have suggestions for rewording or minor revisions.

Time Considerations

The recommended procedure for planning writing schedules is to work backward from the date thesis copies are due in the graduate office, setting deadlines for each step leading to that date. It is endemic among graduate students that they do not plan for unforeseen occurrences, which inevitably upset the best-planned schedules. Wise students build allowances into each time segment.

First, time should be budgeted for the typist to make corrections following the oral defense. This sets the latest date for the examination. Working backward from the examination date, the student must plan sufficient time for the examining committee to study the thesis thoroughly. Universities often set minimum periods. A committee must have adequate time to prepare for the examination.[24] Whatever period is established by regulation or directing professor's decision (adjusted always to committee members' personal schedules), sets a deadline for placing final copies in the committee's hands. A sufficient period must be planned prior to the time the committee receives their copies for the typist to type the manuscript, including an allowance for proofreading and correcting errors. With the deadline for placing the final draft in the hands of the typist established, one then works backward to plan for the directing professor to examine the final draft and make his last suggestions. This sets the latest date for completion of the final draft.

24. Although the student might not agree at the time, his efforts are important enough that the committee is obligated to give the best possible examination.

Chapter 9

Accompanying Statements

One or more of the following statements may be required to accompany a thesis when it is submitted to a graduate school. Their order of appearance in a bound thesis varies among universities.

Abstract

Abstracts are concise statements that give the reader an idea of the information contained in the thesis. There are two kinds: descriptive and informative. A descriptive abstract outlines the development of the study— tells what was done, not what the main ideas are. It is a prose table of contents. An informative abstract tells what the study was about. It concentrates on the main ideas, usually in their order of appearance in the thesis. Informative abstracts are more useful than descriptive.

Stipulations are placed on the maximum number of words permitted in abstracts. They must be tightly written precis. A further condensation of a cogently written Summary (q.v.), with the Conclusions (q.v.) and any significant Recommendations (q.v.) incorporated into it, will produce an informative abstract. The investigator also might wish to add a statement about the significance of the study, or its contribution to the discipline.

Vita

A vita is a brief autobiographical sketch that provides some knowledge of the writer's background and qualifications. It is written in outline form in impersonal style. One page should suffice. Items to be included (in their suggested order) are:

Full Name

Date and Place of Birth

Educational Background

Major Area of Special Interest

Vocational and Professional Experience

Membership in Professional and Honorary Societies

Publications

Other Pertinent Information

Copyright Notice

If a student decides to copyright his thesis to show that his interests in the work are reserved, a copyright notice is presented on a separate page, which usually follows the title page. This notice is a simple three-element statement:

the word "Copyright," the abbreviation "Copr.," or the symbol ©;[1]

the full legal name of the author;

the year.

The following form, centered on the page, is recommended for theses:

Copyright by
Gomer Jeffrey Pound
1976

---

1. Use of the symbol © may result in securing copyright in some other countries under provision of the Universal Copyright Convention.

PART II
Reference Guide

Prospectus
(Research Design, Thesis Proposal, Thesis Outline)

Purpose: ☐ to set forth clearly and succinctly what the investigator proposes to do

☐ to seek approval for the proposed study

Evaluation: ☐ cf., Title, p. 69

☐ cf., Approval, p. 70

☐ cf., Introductory Section, p. 73 ff

☐ cf., Appendixes, p. 91

☐ cf., Bibliography, p. 91

☐ cf., Vita, p. 101

☐ cf., General Considerations, p. 93 ff

☐ the general tone is that of a *proposal* (specifically, future tense is employed to describe what the investigator *intends* to do)

☐ the content is organized to present an argument for permission to make the study

Preliminaries

Title

Purpose: ☐ to give a clear, accurate, and concise statement of what was studied

☐ to attract the attention of other scholars who might be interested in the study

Evaluation: ☐ reflects the Statement of the Problem (q.v.)

☐ reflects the Scope and Delimitations (q.v.)

☐ indicates anything that qualifies the Nature and Sources of Data (q.v.)

☐ indicates the Method of Research (q.v.)

☐ promises only what the investigation attempted to fulfill, and no more

☐ includes all terms under which the thesis might be indexed or keyed for information retrieval systems

☐ three or four words or groups of words form the core, with all unnecessary words eliminated.

☐ meaning is clear at a glance, without leaving too much to inference or interpretation

☐ words are well-chosen, stating exactly what is intended, with no terms that have been qualified in an unusual way in the Definition of Terms (q.v.)

☐ construction sounds euphonious, not awkward or contrived, when read aloud

Approval

Purpose: ☐ to provide for signatures of those responsible for final approval of the thesis

Evaluation: ☐ follows the form prescribed by the school to whom the thesis is being submitted

Acknowledgments

Purpose: ☐ to acknowledge assistance in the nature of encouragement, financial aid, permission to use materials, clerical help, cooperation, or proofreading

Evaluation: ☐ only those to whom special indebtedness is owed are mentioned

☐ wording is dignified and in good taste

Preface
(Foreword)

Purpose: ☐ to identify the particular audience to whom the thesis is directed

☐ to express the writer's personal interest in the problem

☐ to state the scope, aim, and general character of the study

☐ to identify the limitations of the material presented

☐ to explain what the investigator wished to accomplish

Evaluation: ☐ includes only material that is in keeping with the character of a thesis (the first two purposes ordinarily are not appropriate)

☐ includes no material that properly belongs in the Introductory Section (q.v.) (the last three purposes ordinarily are fulfilled in the Introductory Section)

Table of Contents
(Contents)

Purpose: ☐ to provide an outline of the material

☐ to enable the reader to estimate the subject matter and scope of the thesis

☐ to provide for convenient reference by page number

Evaluation: ☐ the orders of subtitles (first, second, or third) sufficiently fulfill the first two purposes (ordinarily, the longer the thesis, the more orders of headings)

☐ chapter and lower order titles are explicit and self-sufficient in terms of the study

☐ all captions of the same order bear the same relative importance to the thesis

☐ captions of the same order are placed into parallel construction

☐ all captions match exactly in wording with those in the body of the thesis

☐ page numbers are accurate

Lists of Tables, Figures, and Illustrations
(Tables, Figures, Illustrations, Plates)

Purpose: ☐ to list all displays of data presented in tabular form

☐ to list all illustrative material used in the thesis

Evaluation: ☐ captions are explicit and self-explanatory in terms of the text

☐ captions match exactly in wording with those in the text

☐ captions which are related by a common idea are placed into parallel construction by virtue of that idea

☐ page numbers are accurate

☐ all tables are placed into a separate list

☐ several illustrations of any one kind (ten or more is a good guide) are placed into a separate list

☐ every table, figure, or illustration is listed

Introductory Section

Background Basic to the Problem
(Setting for the Problem, no caption)

Purpose: ☐   to acquaint the reader with the area in which the problem lies

            ☐   to present a brief history of the problem

            ☐   to bring in relevant information which leads to the Statement of the Problem (q.v.)

            ☐   to bring in relevant information which leads to identification of a Need for the Study (q.v.)

            ☐   to suggest reasons for establishing the Scope and Delimitations (q.v.)

            ☐   to relate the present discussion to previous studies

Evaluation: ☐   clearly identifies an area in which a problem exists

            ☐   assumes that the reader is *not* already well-acquainted with the general area in which the problem lies

            ☐   makes a logical transition from the Title (q.v.) to the Statement of the Problem (q.v.)

Statement of the Problem
(The Problem, Problem Statement, Research Questions)

Purpose: ☐   to provide a clear and complete statement of a problem

73

Evaluation: ☐ states an actual problem, not a Purpose of the Study (q.v.) or a Method of Research (q.v.)

☐ can be recast as a valid research question

☐ elaborates the Title (q.v.)

☐ tells succinctly *what* was studied

☐ breaks a complex problem into specific subproblems

Need for the Study
(Significance of the Problem, Significance of the Study,
Justification for the Study)

Purpose: ☐ to point up the area of need for which answers are not obvious

☐ to state reasons *why* the study was undertaken

☐ to validate or justify the problem

☐ to point out the significance of the problem

☐ to point out the relationship of the problem to the world at large

Evaluation: ☐ provides logical reasons for making the study

☐ presents discriminately selected reasons that establish the importance of the problem

☐ develops needs suggested in the Background Basic to the Problem (q.v.)

☐ receives support from the Review of Related Literature (q.v.)

☐ cites authorities who share the investigator's conviction of need

74

Purpose of the Study
(Objectives of the Study)

Purpose: ☐ to suggest what might be accomplished by finding an answer to the Statement of the Problem (q.v.)

☐ to state the objectives of the study

☐ to indicate the probable value of the study

Evaluation: ☐ adequately purports to help overcome the Need for the Study (q.v.)

☐ differentiates between primary and secondary purposes

☐ falls within the Scope and Delimitations (q.v.)

Scope and Delimitations
(Delimitations)

Purpose: ☐ to define clearly the extent of the problem to be investigated

☐ to reject all irrelevant or unwanted aspects of the field in which the study lies

☐ to carefully close all avenues which do not bear directly on the problem and which, if left open, could weaken the study

Evaluation: ☐ all variables to be considered are carefully included

☐ all variables not to be considered are carefully excluded

☐ all variables which are necessary to fulfill the Purpose of the Study (q.v.) are included

☐ reasons for delimitation are suggested by material presented in the Background Basic to the Problem (q.v.)

☐ reasons for delimitation are suggested by the Review of Related Literature (q.v.)

☐ the problem is sufficiently delimited to make a thorough study possible, but not too delimited to warrant an investigation.

Basic Assumptions
(Statement of Assumptions, Research Assumptions, Assumptions)

Purpose: ☐ to state the assumptions upon which the investigation rested

☐ to explain why these assumptions have been accepted in preference to others that might exist

Evaluation: ☐ these assumptions are tenable

☐ these assumptions are in keeping with existing knowledge

☐ these assumptions are supported by other research (cf., Review of Related Literature)

☐ acceptance of these assumptions is a requisite for accepting the Statement of the Hypothesis (q.v.)

☐ these assumptions are used later to interpret data in the Presentation, Analysis, and Interpretation of Data (q.v.)

☐ proper interpretation of the Conclusions (q.v.) is contingent upon acceptance of these assumptions

☐ proper interpretation of the Recommendations (q.v.) is contingent upon acceptance of these assumptions

Statement of the Hypothesis
(Basic Hypothesis)

Purpose: ☐ to propose a probable solution to the Statement of the Problem (q.v.)

76

☐ to enable the reader to follow better the development of the argument in the Presentation, Analysis, and Interpretation of Data (q.v.)

Evaluation: ☐ falls within the Scope and Delimitations (q.v.)

☐ stems from known facts (cf., Review of Related Literature and Background Basic to the Problem) and Basic Assumptions (q.v.)

☐ broken up into subhypotheses, if complex; or, subhypotheses are proposed as solutions to subproblems (cf., Statement of the Problem)

☐ used to help organize the Presentation, Analysis, and Interpretation of Data (q.v.)

☐ proposes statements whose acceptance or rejection form the principal Conclusions (q.v.) of the study

Review of Related Literature
(Survey of Related Literature, Summary of Related Literature, Analysis of Related Studies, Historical Aspects of the Problem)

Purpose: ☐ to present a brief history of studies related to the problem

☐ to acquaint the reader with the present status of the problem

☐ to help establish the limits of the investigation

☐ to suggest methods of research applicable to solving the problem

☐ to provide ideas, theories, hypotheses, and materials which have relevance for the solution to the problem

Evaluation: ☐ each item relates clearly to the problem

☐ items support the Statement of the Problem (q.v.)

- ☐ items support the Need for the Study (q.v.)

- ☐ items support the Scope and Delimitations (q.v.)

- ☐ items support the Basic Assumptions (q.v.)

- ☐ items support the Statement of the Hypothesis (q.v.)

- ☐ items support the Method of Research (q.v.), Research Techniques (q.v.), and Procedures (q.v.)

- ☐ items support the Definition of Terms (q.v.)

- ☐ comparative data, useful in the Presentation, Analysis, and Interpretation of Data (q.v.), are offered (these items are referred to later in the thesis)

- ☐ contrary opinions are reported

- ☐ reliable authorities are cited

- ☐ items are grouped by date, purpose, similarity of population, or contribution to the study

- ☐ a separate chapter is used for the Review, if the number of items warrant it

Nature and Sources of Data

Purpose:
- ☐ to state what kind of data were sought

- ☐ to state a rationale for the kind of data sought

- ☐ to advise the reader in what form data were obtained

- ☐ to advise the reader of where, when, and from whom data were obtained

Evaluation:
- ☐ choices of data are appropriate to solving the Statement of the Problem (q.v.)

□ choices of data are in accordance with the Purpose of the Study (q.v.)

□ choices of data fall within the Scope and Delimitations (q.v.)

□ differentiation is made between primary, secondary, and tertiary sources

□ the nature and sources of all information found in the Presentation, Analysis, and Interpretation of Data (q.v.) are covered in a general way

□ identifying information about all sources of data is found either in the Bibliography (q.v.) or in Appendixes (q.v.)

Method of Research
(Research Design)

Purpose: □ to state the type of research employed in the study

Evaluation: □ is appropriate to solving the Statement of the Problem (q.v.)

□ is appropriate to the Purpose of the Study (q.v.)

□ is appropriate to testing the Statement of the Hypothesis (q.v.)

□ is appropriate to the kind of data sought (cf., Nature and Sources of Data)

□ is suggested by the Review of Related Literature (q.v.)

□ reasons for the choice are made clear

Research Techniques

Purpose: □ to advise the reader of the research techniques employed for the study

Evaluation: ☐ are appropriate to the Method of Research (q.v.)

☐ are appropriate to the Nature and Sources of Data (q.v.)

☐ are appropriate to finding a solution to the Statement of the Problem (q.v.)

☐ can test adequately the Statement of the Hypothesis (q.v.)

☐ are suggested by the Review of Related Literature (q.v.)

Procedures

Purpose: ☐ to advise the reader of the sequence of steps followed during the study, or of the research design employed

Evaluation: ☐ are in accordance with the Research Techniques (q.v.)

☐ are in accordance with the Method of Research (q.v.)

☐ are appropriate to the Nature and Sources of Data (q.v.)

☐ are suggested by the Review of Related Literature (q.v.)

Definition of Terms

Purpose: ☐ to define terms which are
unique to the study
used in a restricted manner
used with a meaning different from usual
technical
coined by the investigator

Evaluation: ☐ authority is cited for all definitions, except for terms coined by the investigator

☐ terms are defined in words other than themselves

☐ terms are defined in words simpler than themselves

80

☐ definitions state what terms mean, rather than what they do not mean

☐ these terms are used consistently in their defined meanings throughout the remainder of the thesis

☐ terms defined in this section are used in their generally accepted sense if found earlier in the thesis

☐ all terms encountered in the remainder of the thesis which require definition are defined at this point

☐ coined terms are logical and defensible

List of Abbreviations

Purpose: ☐ to set forth a list of abbreviations to be used for convenience of reference throughout the remainder of the thesis

Evaluation: ☐ these are standard abbreviations, accepted within the discipline

☐ these abbreviations are employed consistently throughout the remainder of the thesis

☐ these abbreviations are not used prior to their introduction in this list

☐ all abbreviations unique to the study that occur in the remainder of the thesis are included in this list

☐ abbreviations set up by the investigator are logical and not likely to be confused with other abbreviations

Organization of the Remainder of the Report

Purpose: ☐ to prepare the reader for the way in which the material he will be reading is organized

Evaluation: ☐ does not anticipate actual data

Presentation, Analysis, and Interpretation of Data

Presentation and Analysis of Data

Purpose:
☐ to bring all available pertinent data to bear on the problem

☐ to describe exactly what data were collected, where, how, and when they were located, and how and in what form they were obtained

☐ to describe what steps were taken to validate all data, what safeguards were made against possible errors in collecting and organizing the evidence

☐ to describe any equipment or apparatus used in the study

☐ to describe what analytical treatments were given the data, and what the results of these treatments were

Evaluation:
☐ primary sources have been drawn upon as the principal sources of data whenever feasible

☐ all obvious sources of data are included

☐ sources of data are informed

☐ sources of data are competent

☐ sources of data are unbiased (or, their bias is taken into account)

- ☐ data are accurate (their accuracy has been confirmed)

- ☐ data are reliable (their reliability has been tested)

- ☐ data are valid (their validity has been tested)

- ☐ all data bear on the problem, with irrelevant information removed

- ☐ data are complete enough to fulfill the Purpose of the Study (q.v.)

- ☐ all data fall within the Scope and Delimitations (g.v.)

- ☐ data are adequate enough to test the Statement of the Hypothesis (q.v.)

- ☐ reasons are given for the choices of analytical treatments

- ☐ arguments both pro and con are presented

- ☐ data and their treatment are presented in such detail that others can replicate the study and verify its findings

- ☐ data are well-documented (cf., Documentation)

- ☐ important statements or points that bear on the problem are not outdated

- ☐ direct quotations are used judiciously

- ☐ suitable displays of data are used

- ☐ displays are clear, accurate, and effective

- ☐ each display is self-contained, with a title and explanation of its symbols and how information is to be read

- ☐ each display deals with one main idea

- ☐ each display is introduced with a sentence or two in the text

☐ each display appears as close as physically possible to its introduction

☐ each display is followed by a comment or two about what it reveals

☐ each display is listed in an appropriate list following the Table of Contents (q.v.)

Interpretation of the Data

Purpose: ☐ to give the reader a more informative interpretation of the results of the analysis of data than he can find elsewhere

Evaluation: ☐ data are interpreted accurately

☐ data are interpreted logically

☐ data are interpreted objectively, without hint of bias

☐ interrelationships are pointed out, both among the findings and with other studies (cf., Review of Related Literature)

☐ "blind spots" or gaps in the data are accounted for

☐ alternative explanations have been considered

☐ data are interpreted in light of accepting or refuting the Statement of the Hypothesis (q.v.)

Organization of the Data

Purpose: ☐ to develop the argument clearly, logically, and coherently

Evaluation: ☐ this organization is appropriate to the Method of

85

Research (q.v.), Research Techniques (q.v.), and Procedures (q.v.)

☐ this organization is designed to bring arguments to bear
on the Statement of the Hypothesis (q.v.)

☐ data are presented in an unbiased arrangement

☐ data are organized so as to lead logically to the
Conclusions (q.v.)

Concluding Section

Summary

Purpose: ☐   to review briefly the entire thesis up to this point

Evaluation: ☐   this is a synopsis of the entire content of the preceding portions of the thesis

                  ☐   this is an incisive condensation and synthesis of chapter summaries (if chapter summaries are used), rather than a repetition of previous summaries

                  ☐   an Abstract (q.v.), exclusive of Conclusions (q.v.) and Recommendations (q.v.) can be extracted easily from this summary

                  ☐   only material previously presented is reviewed, with *no* new information introduced

Conclusions

Purpose: ☐   to draw conclusions on the basis of the data presented

Evaluation: ☐   the chief conclusion is a response to the Statement of the Hypothesis (q.v.), with other conclusions responding to subhypotheses

                  ☐   the conclusions provide answers to the Statement of the Problem (q.v.), or reject untenable answers

                  ☐   the conclusions satisfy the Purpose of the Study (q.v.)

87

☐ the conclusions relate closely to the Title (q.v.): they do not suggest that the study has deviated from its original intent

☐ all assumptions necessary to accept the conclusions have been previously set forth in Basic Assumptions (q.v.)

☐ any generalizations to other populations or situations made by these conclusions do not exceed the Scope and Delimitations (q.v.)

☐ each conclusion can be justified by data previously made known to the reader

☐ these conclusions interpret the results, they do not repeat the findings

☐ good logic has been employed

☐ these conclusions are free from mere opinion

☐ these conclusions can explain all the data

☐ these conclusions explain the data better than others

☐ premature conclusions have been avoided

☐ adverse evidence has been considered

☐ these conclusions are stated clearly

☐ violent, dramatic, or emotional terms, which suggest bias and poor scholarship, have been avoided

Recommendations
(Implications of the Research)

Purpose: ☐ to suggest how the knowledge or information obtained might be put to use

☐ to propose further lines of investigation suggested by the study

88

☐ to list unanswered questions which occurred to the investigator, but require research beyond the limits of the undertaking reported

Evaluation: ☐ they relate back to fulfillment of the Purpose of the Study (q.v.) and the Need for the Study (q.v.)

☐ they are stated clearly as opinion and not as additions to knowledge

☐ they are feasible and practical

☐ they do not exceed the Scope and Delimitations (q.v.)

☐ they are not likely to produce unforeseen and undesirable by-products

☐ they really are warranted

Limitations of the Study
(Interpretative Precautions, Cautions for Use of the Study, Observations)

Purpose: ☐ to give suggestions or cautions to be followed for use of the study

☐ to point out the shortcomings, limitations, or weaknesses of the study

☐ to give suggestions helpful to another scholar who might undertake a similar project

Evaluation: ☐ apologetic terms are avoided

☐ hedge words are avoided

Reference Section

Appendixes

Purpose: ☐ to present important related material that does not fit into the main body of the thesis, or will detract from clarity and directness of communication

☐ to furnish raw data and documents which are not readily accessible for a check on the reliability of the study, and to make this information available for future use

Evaluation: ☐ each category of material forms a separate appendix

☐ each appendix has relevance to some part of the body of the thesis (it is referred to at least once in the main text)

Bibliography
(Selected Bibliography, Bibliography of Cited Works, Sources Consulted)

Purpose: ☐ to furnish descriptive details for all useful sources of data

☐ to help other scholars who are working on related studies build a working bibliography

Evaluation: ☐ each entry can be justified on the basis of actual contribution to the study

☐ all necessary information is included for each entry

☐ sources are up-to-date in terms of the problem area

- [ ] all basic sources in the problem area appear

- [ ] primary sources are represented as much as it is possible

- [ ] sources are reliable

- [ ] sources are valid

- [ ] all footnote sources appear

- [ ] entries are classified according to type of publication or character of other sources (unless the Bibliography is very short)

- [ ] there is no evidence of "padding" or inflating the list

General Considerations

Documentation

Purpose: ☐   to establish authority for facts or opinions

Evaluation: ☐   authority is cited for every fact that is not widely known, contradictory to other facts, difficult to verify, or otherwise might be open to question

               ☐   authority or source is cited for every opinion or conclusion taken from publications, interviews, or other sources

               ☐   every direct quotation is documented

               ☐   every source cited in footnotes is found in the Bibliography (q.v.)

Organization of the Thesis

Purpose: ☐   to make content intelligible

Evaluation: ☐   the thesis follows the accepted order for presenting all material (deviations are defensible)

               ☐   organization is clear and logical

               ☐   a complete preview of the study is given in the Introductory Section (q.v.)

- [ ] each chapter, exclusive of the first and last, opens with a paragraph or two containing
  a statement of the portion of the problem to which the chapter is devoted
  a description of the materials and methods used in this part of the investigation
  an enumeration of points to be covered

- [ ] each chapter, exclusive of the first and last, contains a suitable summary, indicating its contribution to the whole study

- [ ] good sentence sense is evidenced
  all sentences are complete
  each sentence contains one idea (if more than one, they are properly subordinated)
  all sentences express a connected thought
  clauses are properly placed
  sentences which are either quite short or unusually long are used sparingly

- [ ] good paragraph sense is evidenced
  each paragraph has a topic sentence either stated or implied, with its thought developed to form a paragraph
  paragraphs maintain their internal unity
  transitions are made between successive paragraphs
  one sentence paragraphs, although permissible when warranted, are found infrequently

- [ ] the most important elements of each sentence, paragraph, or section are given emphasis through placement, constructional techniques, or devices of format

- [ ] an outline of each section can be derived easily

- [ ] the thesis can be read discontinuously

Vocabulary

Purpose: - [ ] to transmit information efficiently and unequivocably

Evaluation: ☐ vocabulary is clear, straightforward, effectively selected, unpretentious, accurate, and precise

☐ words are used for their denotative, not their connotative, value

☐ a standard dictionary is the authority for all meanings

☐ the level of usage is scholarly, with obsolete, obsolescent, or rare usages avoided

☐ pedantry is avoided without resorting to the level of common speech

☐ conversational modes are avoided

☐ descriptive adjectives and adverbs of manner or degree are treated cautiously

☐ hedge words are avoided

☐ euphemisms are avoided

☐ cliches and mannerisms are avoided

☐ jargon, slang, vulgarisms, and colloquialisms are eliminated (unless used for a particular purpose and clearly identified for what they are)

☐ words suggesting dogmatism are avoided

☐ positive words suggesting an exaggerated sense of self-assurance are avoided

☐ frequent repetition of words or phrases is avoided

Spelling

Purpose: ☐ to insure that the words selected are presented correctly

Evaluation: ☐ spellings are orthodox (not shortened) and accurate, with the dictionary as authority

☐ spellings are consistent

☐ all abbreviations are approved by the style manual or set up in the List of Abbreviations (q.v.) (contractions are abbreviations and, as such, are not appropriate for formal style)

Grammar

Purpose: ☐ to be absolutely clear in statement

Evaluation: ☐ subjects of sentences usually are stated directly, without an overuse of introductory clauses

☐ all modifiers—words, phrases, clauses—link properly with the words they modify

☐ attributive nouns are used carefully

☐ pronouns are used discriminately, and refer to their proper antecedents

☐ subjects and verbs agree

☐ adjectives are not used as adverbs, or vice-versa

☐ there are no unnecessary shifts in person, number, tense, or case

☐ parallelism is used correctly

☐ verbs are not split

☐ double negatives are avoided

Punctuation

Purpose: ☐ to clarify the written expression

Evaluation: ☐ readers can interpret each sentence *only* as the writer intended

☐ subordinate material is set off with commas

☐ commas set off each item in a series

Person

Purpose: ☐ to conform with formal style of expression

Evaluation: ☐ third person is employed exclusively (except in direct quotations)

Tense

Purpose: ☐ to report what *has transpired*

Evaluation: ☐ past tense is employed consistently to report the study

☐ present tense is limited to "timeless truths"

☐ future tense is used only to refer within the thesis itself

Voice

Purpose: ☐ to create directness in statement

☐ to avoid wordiness

☐ to enliven the discourse

Evaluation: ☐ active voice predominates

Brevity

Purpose: ☐ to achieve economy of expression

Evaluation: ☐ only (but all) content necessary for understanding the study is included

☐ all unnecessary words have been eliminated

☐ there are no needless repetitions

Revision

Purpose: ☐ to produce a highly refined and polished document

Evaluation: ☐ character and tone are consistent throughout

☐ thought flows logically

☐ there is variety in vocabulary, sentences, and paragraphs

☐ the manuscript has been put aside for a time before final revision

☐ the manuscript has been read aloud

Format

Purpose: ☐ to make the content psychologically more effective

☐ to enhance the physical appearance of the thesis

☐ to check on internal matters of style

Evaluation: ☐ all matters of form adhere to the prescribed style manual (deviations are defensible)

☐ form is consistent throughout

☐ headings are adequate

☐ footnotes are not excessive

☐ quotations are not too long or too frequent

☐ techniques of format that set off important ideas are used effectively

☐ sentences and paragraphs show variety in length

Proofreading

Purpose: ☐ to assure that the final copy is accurate and correct in every detail

Evaluation: ☐ someone other than the writer carefully proofreads the thesis

☐ the typist's clean copy is compared exactingly to the final draft

☐ proofreading is done in several short sittings

Time Considerations

Purpose: ☐ to insure that the thesis will be ready on or before the deadline for submission to the graduate office

Evaluation: ☐ a calendar has been devised which establishes time frames for each important step leading to the deadline for submission to the graduate office

☐ allowances for unanticipated delays are built into each time segment

Accompanying Statements

Abstract

Purpose: ☐ to tell in a few words what the study was about

Evaluation: ☐ covers the Statement of the Problem (q.v.)

☐ covers the Statement of the Hypothesis (q.v.)

☐ indicates the Scope and Delimitations (q.v.)

☐ outlines the Method of Research (q.v.), Research Techniques (q.v.), and Procedures (q.v.)

☐ reports the principal findings

☐ reports the Conclusions (q.v.)

☐ reports the Recommendations (q.v.), if they are important

☐ follows the prescribed form

☐ is under the maximum number of words permitted

Vita

Purpose: ☐ to provide a brief autobiographical sketch of the writer's background and qualifications

Evaluation: ☐ information is in outline form

- [ ] wording is impersonal

- [ ] only pertinent personal information is included

Copyright Notice

Purpose: - [ ] to protect certain exclusive rights in the thesis, as given by copyright law

Evaluation: - [ ] follows the form required by copyright law

Index